Good News Club Series

Street Games

by Kathryn Dahlstrom

Good News Clubs®,
weekday Bible clubs for boys and girls,
are sponsored by
Child Evangelism Fellowship® Inc.

Published by
CEF PRESS®
P. O. Box 348
Warrenton, MO 63383-0348

2 3 4 5 6 — 01 00 99 98 97

ISBN 1-55976-829-0

Kids
everywhere

meet once a week to hear
Bible stories, sing, play games
and have a great time.

Where do they go?

Good News Club!

If you're between
5 and 12 years old and would like
to join a Good News Club near you, call:
1-800-300-4033

That's the number for USA Ministries at Child Evangelism Fellowship.
They sponsor Good News Clubs and can tell you
everything you need to know.

"Home run, Carlos!"

"Hit it to the ocean, man!"

"Nah! Slam it into outer space!"

His teammates' shouts of encouragement caused Carlos Hernandez to lock his teeth together in an eager, wild-eyed grin. He stretched out his left arm in front of him and balanced a beat-up soccer ball on his upturned palm. He bent his right arm back and formed a tight fist.

"Back up, you guys!" hollered the other team's captain with a swift glance over her shoulder. She was playing third base. Her entire team, even the kids who were supposed to be guarding the other bases, moved backwards several steps.

A wave of exultation passed over Carlos. They were *scared* of him! And well they should be. He could punch the ball farther than anyone on his team. And the captain had a right to be worried. The bases were loaded.

"Hrrnngg!" He slammed his fist into the ball with a grunt as mighty as his effort. It flew toward center field and he raced for first base. The air vibrated with the gutsy cheers of his teammates and the screams of the opposing players. "Get it in! Throw it *in!* Here! *HERE!"*

Carlos jetted around first and took a quick glance at the ball chasers' progress. He'd sent the ball far over the infield players' heads; it landed beyond the center fielder's reach, and half their team, it seemed, was running after it—the entire outfield, a couple of base players, and the shortstop too.

Second base was left completely unguarded. He crossed it with a chuckle. The captain frantically covered third, screaming orders the entire time. "Here! Throw it to *me-e-e-e!"*

His team's three base runners were already safe at home. He tore around third. Out of the corner of his right eye he saw a blur of black and white. Someone had hurled the soccer ball to the captain, who caught it on the bounce and began chasing him, bent on tagging him out.

Carlos pushed himself to the top of his speed, but she had longer legs than he did—she was in the *other* fifth grade class at Fern Street Elementary—and she was gaining on him. He still had half the distance to go! What was worse, the boy who played first base (his name was Jose, pronounced Hoh-ZAY) had scrambled to cover home. "Throw it to me, Tamyra!" he yelled.

Tamyra threw the ball past Carlos' head. Drat! The first baseman caught it and planted himself on home plate with the ball outstretched and a scowl on his face, ready to tag him out. If he stopped running, they'd only get him in a rundown. These two were too good to get wild and drop the ball.

Sliding was his only option, but he'd never tried it before. He pictured how a major league baseball player did it and hoped it wouldn't hurt. Then he turned sideways and skidded his feet out from under him.

O-w-w! Carlos' shirt lifted up and the bare skin on his right side scraped against dirt and grass. His elbow smacked the ground hard. But worst of all, his feet hit Jose's ankles and knocked him over.

O-o-f! Jose's chest slammed onto his face, crushing his nose and making the world dark for one awful second. The weight crushed his air away. Then the kid shoved himself to his feet and Carlos felt something hard thump against his shoulder.

"OUT!" bellowed Tamyra and Jose at the same time.

Carlos' teammates—they called themselves the Good News Club—rushed to his defense. "He is *not!*" yelled Felipe Delgado (pronounced Fay-LEEP Dayl-GAH-doh), Carlos' best friend. "He touched home before you tagged him!"

Jose planted the ball in the crook of his arm and stuck his chest out at Felipe. "He is too! He ain't touching no plate, and I just got 'im!"

Mashell (pronounced Muh-SHELL) Robertson, one of the older members of the Good News Club—she was twelve—joined the argument. Her head wagged and she had one eyebrow raised, putting a curved crease in her dark brown forehead. "Once you touch home, you already safe!"

"He never stepped on it!" hollered Tamyra with the same mannerisms as Mashell. "He hit Jose's feet!"

Felipe's voice was getting louder with each phrase. "He did *too!* He slid right across the plate as big buffalo Jose fell on him!"

Jose made a grab for Felipe's shirt. "You callin' me a *name,* man?"

Felipe smacked his hand away and said, "No. Just stating a fact."

They probably would have wound up in an all-out fight
if Carlos hadn't groaned, "I don't care if I'm out or safe!
Just help me up sometime before next Tuesday. I feel like
all my ribs are broken!"

His friends rushed to pull him to his feet and brush the
dirt off his clothes. Suddenly he heard a chorus of teenage
voices behind him, clapping and whistling and shouting.
"Sign him *up,* man! With a punch like that, he could win
the world fistball championships!"

Carlos turned to see his admirers and his face flushed
red. Oh! It was only his brothers, Ricardo and Luis, and
their friends, eight young men with teasing eyes and broad
grins on their faces. They all wore baggy jeans, but none of
their shirts matched and they didn't wear their jet black
hair the same. They weren't in a street gang, and Carlos
was *glad.*

They were just having fun with him. He seriously
doubted they meant their compliments, but he didn't mind
hearing them, all the same. "You be sure and give me a ride
in your new sports car when they give you a million-dollar
contract, okay Carlos?" said fifteen-year-old Luis
(pronounced Loo-EECE).

Ricardo, seventeen, smacked Luis' shoulder. "What are you talking about? He's gonna make you his chauffeur!"

"You get to drive him to McDonalds for a burger, man!" added another teen. "And keep him supplied with comic books!"

The teens strolled away from the kids with their constant teasing now focused on Luis, who gave back insults as fast as he got them. Felipe pulled the young fistball players back to the matter at hand. "It *was* a great hit, man!" he told Carlos with a sharp glance at Jose. "It puts us ahead by three, and we've got two more outs left!"

Jose narrowed his eyes. "You're ahead by two and you've got *one* out left!"

"Two!"

"One!"

"He was safe!"

"Was not!"

Loud, disturbing noises suddenly interrupted their argument. The roar of a car engine speeding up jerked their heads toward the street. Then they heard the screech of tires going around a corner much faster than they were meant to. What followed was worst of all—the popping, explosive cracks of gunshots.

It was a drive-by shooting, aimed at one of the teenage boys. And the kids happened to be caught in the crossfire.

The children screamed and dropped face down on the
ground. Some ducked behind a nearby trash can, others
under the graffiti-painted player's benches. The speeding
car, a brown Chevy Camaro, roared past them with more
gun blasts, then faded away as quickly as it had appeared.

Mashell was the first to cry out. "Anybody *hurt?* Is
everybody alright?"

None of the young fistball players had been hit by
bullets. But as Carlos sat up, he was horrified to see the
teens gathered around one of their friends, lying on his
back. His cries of pain carried across the park. The kids
looked at each other in helpless fear and sympathy.

Except Mashell. She was on her feet, racing toward the
victim and yelling, "Is he *bad?*" The others joined her to
form a silent wall of frightened watchers.

Ricardo didn't answer her. He stood with grim rage in his eyes and yelled, "We gotta get help! We gotta get an ambulance! Call 9-1-1 . . . ."

"*I* will!" One of the teens took off at an all-out run toward the nearest house. "We gotta stop the bleeding," muttered Luis frantically. He yanked off his own T-shirt, ripped it in half, and pressed the wads on his friend's wounds. Ricardo helped him hold the temporary bandages in place. They quickly became soaked with red.

The young man had been hit twice—on the right shoulder and lower arm. Carlos winced in sympathetic pain and rubbed himself in the wounds' locations. And he wasn't even aware he was doing it. The teen moaned and muttered in Spanish and looked at the sky with agony in his eyes. He tried to sit up but Ricardo and Luis held him down.

"Don't move, man, don't move!" Ricardo ordered him. "You're just making yourself bleed more. An ambulance is gonna get here any second, you know? You're gonna be okay. Just lie still."

Luis' eyes were as hard as a statue's and he said quietly, in a voice strained with anger and hurt, "We'll venge (street slang for revenge) you. You hear me? We'll venge you!"

He glared around at the other teens. "You saw the red jackets too, didn't you?"

They nodded and he went on to curdle the air with swear words meant for the group whose red jackets made clear who'd done the shooting: the Blades. The most violent street gang in Los Angeles.

"We're not taking any more from those *asesinos* (murderers, pronounced ah-say-SEE-noce)," said another teen. "It's time to start treating the Blades the way they're treating us!"

"What's their *problem*, attacking us?" blurted out another. "We're not the Knights! We're not any gang at all."

Luis set his jaw. "Maybe we should become one. We've got to protect each other, you know? And venge each other."

The other teens agreed, which made Carlos feel cold inside. And sick. His brothers in a *gang?* He pictured the four Blades he and the other Good News Kids had fought against several months ago. They were vicious. They would have shot a homeless old man and beat up the kids with electric plug-in cords if the police hadn't arrived. They'd kill another human being just for walking on the wrong street. *Their* street. Their turf.

His brothers weren't mean like that. They could *never* be. But once they joined a gang, they'd be drafted into street warfare. They'd start carrying concealed weapons. They'd kill. They'd *be* killed.

He pictured either Ricardo or Luis lying on the ground bleeding and gasping in pain. He had to shut his eyes hard to keep them dry. *No, God, no!* he prayed silently. *Please! They've stayed out of the gangs for so long! Don't let them start now!*

The distant pulse of an approaching siren reminded him to pray for the young man lying in front of him. The ambulance arrived moments before the police did. Soon the teen's wounds were wrapped in white bandages and the emergency medical team was hoisting his stretcher into the ambulance's open back. Meanwhile, the officers plied the others with questions.

"It's the Blades, man! They were all wearing red jackets in the car," Luis kept telling them. "Why don't you throw them all in jail?"

The police finished gathering information and left. They'd completely ignored the Good News Kids and other onlookers.

The gawkers drifted away. The teens stalked off, still vowing revenge. The young fistball players were left to themselves, now glum and subdued. Nobody could remember the game's score. Nobody cared. They didn't want to play anymore, anyway.

* * * * * * * *

Mashell felt sorry for Carlos. She could see worry weighing on him as though he were balancing an invisible boulder across his shoulders. Anna (pronounced AH-nuh), his thirteen-year-old sister, looked worried too. She and Mashell walked ahead of Carlos and Felipe, on their way toward the one bright spot in an otherwise terrible week: Good News Club. It was bound to cheer them up.

They hurried past Gordon Brown's two-story, four-unit apartments—dingy, rectangular buildings with not much space between them. Their back doors opened to common ground covered with patchy, wilted grass. Mashell ignored the scattered litter and the clotheslines draped with laundry. This was home. She'd seen these things all her life.

They raced toward one living unit that had been turned
into a meeting room and pushed through its door to find
their seats. The older kids sat at the fourth long table in the
back of the room. The teachers tried their best to make the
meeting place cheerful by covering the walls' dents and
scuff marks with posters. But they couldn't do anything to
make it less cramped. The thirty or so kids who came each
week barely had room enough to walk between tables and
the teachers always had to be aware of their surroundings or
they'd knock things over.

Which was more amusing than irritating, as far as
Mashell was concerned. She skipped sideways to "her"
folding metal chair and plopped down. (She sat on it every
week and no one contested her for it.) Anna and Carlos and
Felipe followed and two sixth-grade boys—Juan
(pronounced HWAHN) Cortez and Nathaniel Bronson
(Bronce, for short)—greeted them with nods. Mrs. Marge
Joyce was the only teacher present, so far. She was busy
setting up her three-legged visual-aid stand.

She glanced up. "Glad you four came today!" she told
them. Mashell watched her eyes narrow as she observed
Carlos. Then she placed one deep brown arm across her

stomach and planted the other elbow on it so she could tap
her fingers on her chin. The older, middle-aged lady struck
this pose a lot, whenever she had something to ponder. Like
how to get an eleven-year-old boy to tell her what was
bothering him.

"Carlos, how 'bout you help me pick out today's songs?"
she asked him. He rose reluctantly to take on a task the rest
of the kids were *busting* to do. He listlessly pulled out
several song-word posters and started to return to his seat
without a word. But Mrs. Joyce stopped him and Mashell
watched her whisper something in his ear. Probably asking
him if he wanted to talk to her after the club was over.

He shrugged, and that would have been that. But her
question must have trickled out to the young girls at the
front table, who were straining to hear every word she said.
Now, anyway. They rarely paid attention that closely during
the *story*.

Mashell's five-year-old sister, Loeesha (pronounced
Loh-EE-shuh), suddenly spoke loudly and in an "important"
voice. Her head wagged as she talked, and so did the dozen
or so tiny braids all over her head. "Carlos is sad because
he saw somebody get *shot* yesterday. The Blades got his

big brothers' friend in a drive-by. And now he afraid his
brother will go out and shoot somebody *else.*"

Mashell had a strong urge to crawl under the table. *Why*
did she tell Loeesha what happened yesterday? *Why?* She
should have known her little sister would "blab at the mouth."

Carlos reacted as she expected him to—with anger.
"Shut-up, Loeesha! Ricky and Luis never said they'd *shoot*
anybody. Just that they wanted to get revenge for their
friend getting hurt. My brothers ain't *killers!"*

He stomped back to his chair and flopped down.
Mashell didn't dare look at him. Mrs. J clicked her tongue.
"Oh, my, my! You say this happened yesterday?" She
sighed. "Lord Jesus, when's all this violence gonna *end?"*

She took in all the children with a look and Mashell
expected her to give them a patient explanation of what
happened yesterday. Instead, she folded her hands, bowed
her head, and quietly asked the kids to do the same. "Oh,
Lord Jesus," she prayed, "help us! We don't understand
things like this. Why young people—children, really—go
around shooting other children. How it must break Your
heart! But we ask you to teach us *our* part in bringin' peace
to Los Angeles. Fill our hearts with Your love, Lord, 'cause

Your love is the *only* thing that can overcome this hate. In
Jesus' *name* we pray!"

She seemed about to end the prayer, then changed her
mind. "Oh, an' one more thing, Lord. Keep Ricardo and
Luis safe. Keep Carlos, keep these children, keep *all* of us
free from harm. Surround us with Your protecting hands
that we *know* are around us, whether we feel 'em or not.
Thank You, Lord. Amen."

"Amen," echoed the children. Mashell risked a glance
at Carlos and thought sure she saw moisture in his eyes.
But he blinked it away.

The other two Good News Club leaders—blond-haired
Mrs. Nancy Peterson, who was Mrs. Joyce's age, and Miss
Becky Lindstrom, who was in her early twenties—had
slipped into the room during the prayer. Mrs. Peterson
pushed her glasses up on her nose and whistled. "Boys and
girls, I'm amazed at today's Bible story. It's just *exactly*
what we need to hear. I think God wants to tell us
something."

With that, she busied herself pulling out visual aids from
a burgundy briefcase. Mashell, sizzling with curiosity,
wanted to yell out, "So, get *on* with it!"

3

The meeting was officially beginning. Miss Lindstrom, looking as frazzled as usual, flipped her long, auburn ponytail off her shoulder so she could slip on her guitar strap. Then she had to thread her way to the front of the room without bumping the guitar. She didn't make it. It struck a table corner with a sickening *thunk,* and she led the first song with a pained look on her face. No wonder. Mashell could see the fresh nick from where she sat.

The next song went better. And the next one. Mashell enjoyed singing boldly with the others and she and Anna prided themselves on the getting the movements exactly right. In fact, Miss Lindstrom had them stand beside her so the others would get them right, too. But part of her wanted to get *on* with things. What had Mrs. Peterson *meant* when she said God wanted to tell them something?

There weren't any drive-by shootings in the Bible, were there?

At last, Mrs. Peterson stuck four rough-backed paper figures to the flannelboard she'd put on the three-legged stand. They wore long, bright-colored robes—an old man and woman and two young men about Miss Lindstrom's age. "So how does the story of these people who lived thousands of years ago tie into a drive-by shooting here in Watts? Well, let me tell you."

Mashell leaned forward slightly. The room was so quiet a cat walking across the floor would have sounded like a stampeding buffalo. Mrs. Peterson told them that the old people were a married couple named Isaac and Rebekah. Their twin sons were named Esau and Jacob. Esau had been born first—just a few minutes ahead of his brother— and according to ancient custom he was supposed to inherit the control of his father's wealth and property. In other words, when his father died, he, the oldest son, would become head of the family. This custom was called the *birthright*. Esau was also to receive an important spoken gift from his father called his *blessing*.

But when they grew up, Jacob bribed Esau into giving *him*—the younger brother—the birthright. Even worse, Rebekah talked Jacob into tricking Isaac. The old man was nearly blind, so Jacob disguised himself as Esau. Isaac, thinking he was blessing his oldest son, blessed his younger one instead. And once the blessing was given, it couldn't be taken back. Nor could it be given to anyone else. Jacob had stolen the blessing that Esau was supposed to receive.

"When Isaac realized he'd blessed the *wrong* son, he became so upset he shook violently," Mrs. Peterson said, making her body quiver like a person having a seizure. "I bet he almost *died,* poor old man!"

She raised one eyebrow. "And Esau was *furious!* Jacob already had Esau's birthright! *Now* he'd taken his blessing! From now on, he, the older brother, would have to serve and obey the younger! So he vowed to kill Jacob. And he *meant* it!"

She scanned the children, but her gaze settled on the back table. "Now do you see why this story is like yesterday's shooting?"

Mashell raised her hand, then spoke out before receiving permission. She couldn't help it. This topic had her

absolute, burning interest. "Jacob did somethin' really
lowdown. He cheated his brother to get control of the
family money." She paused for a moment. "Which is just
about as bad as shootin' somebody from a car. So Esau
swore he'd get revenge. Just like Ricardo and Luis want."

Mrs. Peterson looked pleased with her answer. "Jacob's
cheating caused a lot of pain to others, didn't it—"

Felipe cut in (with his hand raised, of course). "Just
like that drive-by caused one guy to get shot and lots of
others to get real mad." He glanced at Carlos. "And real
worried."

Mrs. Peterson gained control of the discussion again.
"Next week you'll find out that Jacob's cheating caused *him*
lots of pain, too. In fact—"

"Does Esau *kill* him?" Mashell blurted out.

"Please don't interrupt. You'll find out next week."

The kids groaned and begged, but nothing they said
could make Mrs. Peterson tell them what would happen
next. She wasn't finished teaching, though. "Let me ask
you this. If Esau *did* kill Jacob, would it solve anything?
Somebody answer other than Mashell and Felipe, please."

Mashell flopped her arm on her lap and bit her lip in frustration. "It would give him control of the family money again," answered Bronce.

Mrs. Peterson folded her arms. "You think so? After he murdered his brother?"

"Oh, yeah," murmured Bronce. "He'd prob'ly have to go to jail. Get the death sentence. Electric chair or somethin'."

She corrected him gently. "They didn't have electricity back then. But they would have punished him *somehow*. He probably would have been killed. The point is, if he murdered his brother he'd ruin his own life, wouldn't he?"

The kids agreed.

"And that would only heap more pain on Jacob and Rebekah, right? They'd lose *both* sons. Do you see what I'm saying? Revenge only causes more hurt and brings about more evil." She glanced at the youngest club leader. "Miss Lindstrom, it's time to teach our Bible memory verse. Matthew six, verses fourteen and fifteen."

Miss Lindstrom hurriedly looked up the passage and read out loud, "For if you forgive men when they sin against you, your Heavenly Father will also forgive you.

But if you do not forgive men their sins, your Father will
not forgive your sins."

Mashell winced. *Ooh! Chilling words! If we don't
forgive others, God won't forgive us!* A glance at Carlos
showed her he was feeling the same sober fear she felt. Not
for himself—he wasn't the type to hold a grudge—but for
his brothers. They *had* to forgive the Blades! They *had* to
let go of this *vengeance.*

Anna seemed more cheerful now, but Carlos was just
the opposite. The boulder on his shoulders grew larger. Not
even the review game—tic-tac-toe—cheered him up. The
other kids nearly pulled themselves out of their chairs from
raising their hands so hard. If they were called on and said
the right answer, they shot up to the tic-tac-toe squares and
stuck plastic "X's" or "O's" to them, depending on which
team they were on. The team with the first three X's or O's
in a row won, of course.

Carlos never raised his hand once. His team, the X's,
won, and he didn't seem excited at all. He passed up the
day's snack and didn't bother to pull a small toy from the
prize box on his way out the door. "Don't you want

anything?" Miss Lindstrom called after him in total surprise. "Not even a pencil or a neon yo-yo?"

He didn't answer her. Mashell caught up with him and said, "Hey, you 'bout ready to fall down under all this weight you carryin'. I think you tellin' yourself it up to you to save your brothers, an' if you don't talk them into givin' up the venge, they gonna die or somethin'."

He stopped walking and gave her a shocked glare. She chuckled in triumph. "I *knew* I was readin' you right! Anyhow, you got to give it up, man! Let God take care of it! *You* can't control what your big brothers do! You think they wanna listen to you any more than that Esau guy wanted to obey—what was his younger brother's name?"

"Jacob," said Carlos.

"Yeah. Him." She raised one eyebrow at her friend and let her words sink in.

Felipe and Anna strolled up to them as he said, "But I have to tell Ricardo and Luis the truth, whether they'll listen or not."

Mashell nodded slowly. "Okay, so you do. But don't blame yourself if they don't listen, and don't torture yourself, waitin' around for your *big chance* to talk to 'em. If you supposed to, the time'll be *right*. And meantime, *lighten up!*"

His shoulders seemed to straighten and he almost smiled. Was his invisible weight just a little lighter? She hoped so. She also hoped Ricardo and Luis *would* listen, in spite of what she'd predicted.

* * * * * * * *

Carlos tried to do what Mashell said. He tried to get his mind on other things instead of how he'd word his warning to his brothers. But it wasn't easy. He had no idea *how* he was supposed to "let God take care of it." He began to fret about something else, too. What if his brothers became angry with him for telling them not to venge Rudy, the teen who got shot?

Bedtime finally came. Carlos waited his turn in the bathroom (which took a lot of patience, considering eight people had to use it). But he was used to life with a large family in a small, two-bedroom house.

He couldn't imagine having a bedroom to himself, as some of his classmates did. Or having a bedroom at all, like the one his three sisters were crowded into. He'd always shared a double bed with Luis. Their bed was shoved up against a side wall of the living room. Ricardo slept against the opposite wall, and the three boys had to cram their clothes into a dresser near the kitchen door.

Luis had made it to bed first. Carlos took Peppy outside to "be a good dog" then flopped into bed himself. Peppy lay on the braided oval rug nearby. Ricardo turned out the light.

Carlos was ready to call it a day and wait for a chance to talk to his brothers tomorrow when Luis suddenly whispered, "Hey, Carlos! Did we tell you Rudy's gonna be all right?"

"Really? That's great!" The boy hoped his voice didn't sound as strained as it felt. Having to speak softly helped. If they didn't, they'd raise a yell from Papa in the back bedroom.

"The doctor said he lost a lot of blood, but he's gonna make it," Luis went on. "Gonna have some nasty scars, though." He turned onto his back and stretched his arm

toward the ceiling. The raised hand formed a fist. Carlos
could barely see it in the dim headlight beams that arced
across the room from a passing car. "They're nothing
compared to the scars we're gonna give the Blade who
shot him, though. Not that a corpse would care how his
arm looks."

Carlos swallowed and hoped his voice wouldn't come
out shaky. "Who's 'we'? "

"Our posse."

"Your *what?*"

Luis quickly explained that he and Ricardo and their
friends had formed a sort of gang called a posse, rather than
a full-fledged street gang like the Blades or the Knights.
"We asked ourselves, 'Do we really wanna take orders from
old gang leaders that have become middle-aged drug
dealers? Do we really wanna have to steal and sell drugs
and all that when all we want is *protection?* You know, the
chance to defend ourselves?' So, we became a posse."

Carlos felt relieved. *A posse.* But there was still
the big, nagging issue of vengeance. "Are you gonna
carry weapons?"

"Some. Just to keep ourselves safe."

Carlos took a deep breath. Now was his "big chance." Why did he feel so scared? "But—you're not going out looking for violence, right—?"

"No way! We're not like the Blades. We don't get our jollies out of hurting people."

The boy licked his lips. "So why do you want to venge anybody? That's more violence, isn't it? Isn't one guy getting shot enough?"

He could feel Luis' scowl more than he could see it, and it made him want to bury his head in his pillow. "What are you *saying!* Not *venge Rudy?*" His brother's voice went from a whisper to a near shout. "What kind of friends do you think we *are?* Don't you think we care about his honor any more than *that?*"

Carlos was shivering, yet he felt hot all over. His voice came out in a whimper. "But—Mrs. Peterson told us—"

Luis sat up. *"Mrs. Peterson!"* he said scornfully. "You spend too much time listening to rich ladies who don't know what it's like to live in Watts!"

"But the Bible says—"

"Quiet, you guys!" hissed Ricardo from his bed across the room. "You wanna wake up Papa?" His warning came

too late. Papa's voice bellowed from their parents'
bedroom. "You boys settle down or I'll come out and do it
for you!"

Luis took a moment to glower at his younger brother
before he lay down again. "I think that Bible club is turning
you into a coward," he muttered.

Carlos rested his head on his pillow, wishing he could
wrap it around his whole body. As if it could soothe the
sting of what his brother just said.

4

The next morning's sunshine was pleasant and—normal.
The sun had no idea what Carlos was going through and
what Ricardo and Luis' posse was planning. The two
teenagers hustled to get ready for the two hours of work
they had to put in before their high school classes began.
They had to trim hedges and mow lawns as Papa's assistant
landscapers.

Mama fussed at them for getting up too late to eat a
good, slow breakfast. Luis took a giant bite out of a rolled
up tortilla, kissed her cheek, and ran out the door taking
another bite. The same as every morning. But then he
grabbed the doorway and yanked himself back inside the
living room before the door could close on his fingers.

Carlos was still in his pajamas, sitting sleepily on the
edge of the bed. He caught his brother's eye and quickly

looked away. Luis sat beside him. "Hey you," he began.
"I'm sorry about what I said last night. I, like, let myself
get too hot, you know? You're not a coward, okay? Not
even close. I've seen you do some pretty brave things. So,
I'm sorry, okay?"

Carlos could only give him a quick glance or Luis
would have seen his eyes grow wet. "Yeah, okay. I—knew
you didn't mean it."

Luis shoved him sideways into his wadded blanket, then
tore out the door before Carlos could fling a pillow at him.
The boy laughed; it seemed like the first time in days.
Peppy trotted over to him, wagging his tail, and let his
young
master put his newfound energy to good use on a back scratch.

Carlos felt so good he ate enough breakfast to even
satisfy Mama.

Then he took Peppy on a fast run around the block. The
golden retriever's tongue flapped against his furry cheek—
his way of laughing. He was delighted because his young
master let him gallop, though it meant Carlos had to clutch
his leash and race like a ballplayer trying to beat a throw to
first base. And still he felt that any second Peppy would

yank him off his feet and drag him facedown.

He was totally out of breath by the time they reached the backyard again, but the dog still had energy to spare. As his young master knelt to snap the long yard chain to his collar, Peppy sprang sideways and thumped his master's shoulder with his front paws. *Wrestle!* his eyes begged.

Carlos obliged him, of course. This was part of the routine and both of them knew it. The two became a mixed-up mess of arms and legs and fur and a long, wet tongue—grunting, laughing, huffing, and puffing.

"Carlos! Quit playing! We have to go or we'll be late for school!" Anna's scolding voice cut their wrestling short, as it did every morning. And as always, his sisters were waiting for him at the front sidewalk. Anna was in seventh grade and Maria and Victoria were in first and second. They started the eight-block trudge to school with Peppy's goodbye yips and yelps following them until they were out of earshot. Also as usual.

If everything was this normal, why should Ricardo and Luis be any different? Maybe their high school teachers would give them a big homework assignment. Maybe Papa would have extra work for them to do. Maybe they'd forget about venging Rudy.

The kids reached the Gordon Brown housing
community. Felipe and Mashell and Loeesha were leaning
against the same palm tree they waited under every day. Its
crisscrossed trunk wasn't much wider than one child at its
base and it tapered up, at a slight curve, to a splayed mass of
giant green fronds. Shaggy growth, the color of dead grass,
hung down under the fronds, covering the top third of the
trunk like the curved roof of a straw hut.

The tree was taller than Gordon Brown's two-story
apartments. Carlos, imagining he was a monkey, felt dizzy
at the thought of climbing it. He noticed that someone had
sprayed fresh graffiti on its trunk, to add to dozens of
scrawls that covered it as high as arms could reach.

He felt almost lighthearted by now. Felipe had taken to
telling "knock-knock" jokes lately, and he managed to
snicker unless they were *really* bad.

"Knock-knock!" Felipe began.

"Who's there?" they chorused.

"Dog."

"Dog who?"

"Doggoned if *I* know!"

Only Loeesha laughed at that one. Felipe, undaunted, started another joke that led to the answer "Orange."

"Orange who?"

"Orange you glad I tell knock-knock jokes?"

"NO!" they all exclaimed. Even Loeesha.

Felipe spared them for a while. The roar of passing cars and trucks became too noisy for good conversation, anyway, as they crossed Central Avenue. Carlos took notice, today, of the small, grimy buildings lining the block. They all had iron bars over their doors and windows. They all had graffiti obscuring their hand-painted business names.

The Mexican restaurant had pictures of shrimp and chicken legs and tacos and Spanish words painted on its walls: *mariscos,* (shellfish, pronounced mah-RISS-koce*), pollo (*chicken, pronounced POY-yoh*), tacos.* The thrift shop advertised T-shirts for two dollars. The corner market's windows were covered with neon posters that listed prices for milk and ground beef. He wished he had more than a dime in his pocket. He would have bought a candy bar.

At the next block, Anna turned away from them and loped

down the street that would bring her to Frederick Douglass Junior High School. Her long, black hair bounced, so shiny it glistened. Carlos noticed Mashell watching her with envy in her eyes. "Can't wait 'til I can go to Douglass, too," she muttered. "Then I'll only have to listen to sad jokes part of the way!"

Carlos knew she had many stronger reasons for wanting to get out of elementary school and into the teen world of junior high. At twelve, she was already painting her fingernails and wearing makeup and wrapping her hair up tight in—who knew what those cloth things were? He was glad he didn't have to bother with all that. And he was glad he wasn't a teenager, yet.

"Just for that, I'm gonna tell another one," said Felipe. But he was cut short by a car squealing around the corner ahead of them. They all gasped and looked for things to duck behind. But it roared by them with no gunshots.

"Don't they know better than to scare us just 'cause they late for *work?*" griped Mashell.

They walked on with Carlos' heart still thumping. The image of Rudy lying on the ground filled his mind. And worry for his brothers' safety settled in his stomach like a block of ice. So much for a perfectly normal morning.

* * * * * * * *

"Who wants to play wallball?" the recess director asked
the two fifth grade classes. Exclamations like "Yeah! We
do!" or groans of "I *hate* that game!" burst out from the fifty
or so kids standing against one stretch of the playground's
wire mesh fence. Mid-morning recess period was just
beginning at Fern Street Elementary School.

She quickly divided the willing players into two teams
of ten each—one team from each class—then set up the
other kids at games they preferred.

Felipe put his hand up for a "slap" with Carlos, who did
it automatically and with no enthusiasm. His friend gave
him a narrow-eyed look. "You worried again? Try to get
your mind off your brothers, man! You ain't gonna do 'em
any good and you ain't gonna have no fun, either."

Carlos gave a nod and a sigh. "I know."

"Wallball's your favorite."

Felipe was right. Of all the playground games, this was
the one he threw himself into the hardest. He began to feel
excited, which Felipe must have noticed because he broke
into a grin. They "sized up" the other team. They were
good. The other class's best athletes all seemed in the mood

for wallball today. Tamyra, the fistball captain, and Jose, the first baseman, were together again. They also had a strong, husky boy named Jeffrey. But Carlos wasn't intimidated. He was good, too.

The director, a stocky woman with thick legs and short gray hair, led them to a long bench alongside a lone wall near the edge of the playground. It looked as though someone hadn't gotten around to attaching it to anything. It was a faded peach color and had a black line running across it near the top. It also had three side-by-side, black-edged rectangles painted on it that the players called "windows." They were placed up and down, and the middle one reached the ground. The shorter ones on each side ended a few inches above the concrete; any ball that hit below them was considered too low and out-of-bounds.

A long yellow rectangle—the playing area—was painted on the concrete with two lines running across it. The ball had to land inside its borders or the player was "out."

Like racquetball, a player had to hit a ball (a big, red, rubbery one instead of a tiny, hard, black one) that bounced off the wall. Standing on the serving line, the hitter had to make it bounce once on the pavement and strike the wall

somewhere above the bottom of the side windows. During
tournament play, the player *also* had to land the ball
between the serving line and the other line painted across
the playing area, near its back edge. Or be out.

The object was to *not* get out. Two kids—one from each
team—stood side-by-side within the playing area (the wall
itself marked the top border) and took turns thunking the ball
and sending it into the wall for the other player to hit. The
first one to miss, or to send it out of bounds, or to fail to hit it
either in the air or after one bounce, sat down. The remaining
player was rewarded one point for his or her team. That person
played again, against a different opponent.

The only part Carlos didn't like about the game was the
rule that a winning player could only get three points before
sitting down. He wished that the players who didn't get
"out" could go on playing. He would have been one
of them.

But he could see the fairness of it. Everyone deserved a
turn. The "sit down after three" rule also kept one team
from slaughtering the other—fifty points to three, or
something funny like that. Funny for the winning team,

that is.

He and Felipe sat on the bench with their classmates. "Do you want to play tournament rules?" asked the playground director.

"Nah!" they all answered. Carlos was glad. Not having to land the ball between the two lines on the playing area allowed more strategy. The director picked two people to start—Tamyra and a girl from Carlos' class named Veronica. Tamyra took the first bounce, sent it to the wall at a sharp angle and left Veronica gasping and giggling. She didn't even *try* to hit it! "I thought it was going to go *out!*" she said with a sheepish chuckle.

Carlos tried not to let his irritation show. Never, *never* give up a shot for lost! Especially when playing against somebody as good as Tamyra, who could control the ball so that it landed barely inside the boundary lines.

One point for the other team. Felipe faced her next, and the play lasted a lot longer. Both sides clapped and yelled as the two sent the ball back into the wall again and again. Tamyra was especially good at hitting the ball before it bounced, and Felipe hit the ball hard enough to let her. *Try hitting it easy, just to throw her off,* thought Carlos, wishing he could enter the playing area long enough to whisper in his friend's ear.

Felipe finally hit it out. The ball rocketed off the wall at a sharp angle that threatened to slam into the bench, scattering the waiting players. *"Out!"* yelled the other team while Felipe groaned in disgust and flopped down.

Two points for the other team. Carlos' turn. He stood with his jaw set. Tamyra put the ball into play and he fisted it in a direction that sent the ball to the edge of the playing area—on *his* side. But she made a dive for it and sent it back *hard*. Carlos wound up at the back of the rectangle.

"Hrrnng!" he grunted. The ball came off the wall like a missile. She slammed it in midair and it skimmed his side. He had all he could do to reach it and his momentum sent it thudding off the wall and toward the back boundary line. She raced to meet it, but now she was set up. She gave him a high-bouncer. He tapped it gently. It hit the wall barely above the bottom of the windows. Tamyra shrieked and dashed forward. But she couldn't reach it before the second bounce.

Yes!

Carlos' team cheered. One point for *them*. Jeffrey faced Carlos next, but hit the ball so hard that it bounced somewhere across the playground. No one saw where it landed at first. All the players on the bench had their heads covered.

"Out," said Carlos in an awestruck voice. Jeffrey sat down scowling.

Tie game.

Jose's turn. "Have a seat, Hernandez," he said.

"You." Carlos put the ball in play and it shot from their hands to the ground to the wall and back. Jose especially liked angle shots that hit close to the boundary lines. Carlos was concentrating so hard his teeth were locked together and he thought of nothing but getting to the ball and putting it somewhere Jose couldn't reach.

That's why tripping was such a shock. One split second he was racing for the ball and the next he was flat on his face with throbbing elbows and knee caps. The ball bounced two feet in front of him. Then bounced again and again until someone on the bench jumped up and caught it.

"You okay?" Jose asked him. But he was drowned out by Carlos' team, who stood and yelled a jumble of phrases at the top of their lungs. "You *tripped* him! *Foul! No fair!*

TEACHER!"

The recess director hurried over to them and somehow managed to understand the problem though ten furious kids were talking at once. She quieted them down and set a stern gaze on Jose. "Is this true?"

"I—didn't mean to. I was trying to reach a shot . . . ."

Carlos' team gave disgusted grunts of disbelief. The director let Felipe speak for them. "You were *not!* It was *Carlos'* turn to hit the ball! You ran up behind him and stuck your foot—"

Jose cut him off. "No, no! I said the wrong thing! I didn't mean I was trying to get the *ball!* I meant I was trying to *set up* another shot! I—it was an accident, really!"

His face was red, from more than exertion, it seemed. Carlos and Felipe exchanged looks. A likely story! "You're lying!" muttered Felipe.

"Who made *you* God?" Tamyra demanded angrily.

"Nobody! But we all *saw* what he did and he's too much of a *coward* to admit it!"

The director intervened before a fight could break out. She ruled the round a "no point-er" and picked two new kids to oppose each other. "But it's still my turn!" protested Jose.

"Oh, but Carlos needs bandaging and you're just the man I want as my assistant."

"But I'm telling the *truth!* Really! I ain't lying to you! I didn't mean to trip him!"

"I'm not saying you did. But he *did* get hurt because your foot was in his way. So your *hands* can help doctor him up."

She led both boys toward the building at a brisk walk. Carlos gave Felipe a quick glance over his shoulder and caught a grin from him that was full of indignant triumph. Jose *had* to be lying! And what a lowdown *phony* thing to do!

But at least he couldn't play anymore this recess.

Carlos' stinging knees and elbows only made him angrier. If he hadn't gotten hurt and Jose had stayed in the game, he would have refused to play against him. In fact, he didn't want to play with him, or Tamyra, or any of Jose's friends ever again.

If they had to cheat to win, they were no friends of *his*.

5

Mashell hurried out of school. It wasn't that she didn't like walking with Carlos and Felipe and the three little girls, but she wanted to talk to Anna in private. So she hurried to catch her as classes let out at Frederick Douglass.

She made sure her hair was pulled straight back and smooth and that her makeup looked fresh. Who wanted to look like a frump in front of a school full of teenagers? She reached the broad walkway leading to the peach-colored building just as the students were spilling out the doors in a colorful, noisy throng.

If she hadn't known that Anna always left by the main entrance, she never could have spotted her. Hundreds of young teens cut across the front lawn—which explained the long strips of bare dirt—or passed her on the walkway.

They took as much notice of her as they did of the squashed gum on the concrete.

Mashell knew lots of these faces, but no one seemed to recognize her. *Guess you're too cool for a twelve year old,* she thought in disgust, promising herself she wouldn't act like that when *she* became a teen. The more they ignored her the crankier she felt, until a cheerful voice cut through her gloom and made the world alright again.

"*Hola (*hello, pronounced OH-lah), Mashell!"

"Hi!" Mashell grinned and gave Anna a wave. Three other girls walked with her, and instead of turning up their noses at her, they greeted her warmly and gathered in a semicircle around her.

"We heard you saw a drive-by shooting!" said one of them.

"Yeah. It was pretty bad."

Another spoke up, looking fearful. "Do you duck every time you see a fast car, now?"

"Yeah." Sober silence fell upon the group for a few awkward moments. Mashell changed the subject by complimenting one of the girls on her outfit, which launched the five of them into a discussion about clothes. After several minutes, Anna's three friends left for home, in

the opposite direction from Gordon Brown and the
Hernandez' house.

Mashell knew Anna was too polite to ask what she was
doing here, so she volunteered the information. "I wanted
to talk to you for a minute without the boys an' the little
girls around. See, Carlos was all worried yesterday 'cause
he was gonna try talkin' Luis into droppin' the venge. Did
he do it? Did he talk to 'im?"

Anna shrugged. "I can't get Carlos to tell me anything,
and I'm just as worried as he is!" Her forehead wrinkled
into a brooding scowl. "Why do there have to be street
gangs, anyway? Why can't everybody just leave everybody
else *alone?*"

Mashell was about to give a sympathetic answer, but she
caught sight of someone who took her breath away. She
gripped Anna's arm and nodded toward the approaching
stranger—and saw fear come across her friend's face. Both
girls pretended to look at their shoes but raised their eyes
enough to watch him.

He was a high schooler, sauntering across the grass as
though his father owned it. He had to be at least seventeen.
He stood nearly two feet taller than the junior highers (who

scattered out of his way), and his chest and arms were broad and bulging with muscles. *Really buff!* thought Mashell, not because she admired his build but because she was scared of him.

The older teen was obviously a homeboy (a member of the neighborhood street gang), one of the Blades. He was wearing a white muscle shirt and she could clearly see a thick-handled, pointed knife, blade down, tattooed on his upper arm and chest. His hair was slicked back and he wore black sunglasses and baggy jeans.

He pushed through a row of gnarled, shiny-leafed bushes growing alongside the school building and followed the wall to the corner where the front entry jutted out. Then he leaned his left shoulder against the bricks and crossed his arms. *Who he waitin' for?* Mashell wondered. Her heart began to beat faster.

Her question was answered in the next moment. A young teen—fourteen or fifteen years old—strolled out the main doors. He had his hair slicked back too, and he was wearing an oversized white T-shirt and similar baggy jeans. He looked like a bony scarecrow compared to the waiting Blade. He didn't have any tattoos either, that Mashell could see. *Must be a wannabe* (someone who wants to be in a gang, but hasn't been accepted yet), she told herself. He hadn't yet noticed the gang member, waiting in the building's shadow like a hungry tiger.

The Blade hissed something, probably the wannabe's name, though Mashell couldn't hear what he said. The kid turned and Mashell was certain she saw fear cross *his* face too—fear that he quickly covered over with a grin and a spoken greeting. The older teen beckoned him to the corner and as they spoke together, the terror that had flickered over the kid's face took over and showed clearly.

And then the wannabe blurted out something that turned her heart to ice. *"The Hernandez brothers! They're out to get me?"*

He must have done the shooting during the drive-by! she thought, forming her hand into a fist. The Blade ordered him to keep his voice down.

If only she could hear what they were talking about! She wished she could turn herself into a moth and fly to the wall beside them. Wait . . . there was a large classroom window just to the right of the Blade's shoulder. And it was open!

A frightening idea popped in her head. She narrowed
her eyes at Anna and spoke hardly louder than a breath.
"We gotta hear what they sayin'. Somethin' about your
brothers! Let's go in that classroom an' listen through the
open window."

Silent tears were bubbling from Anna's eyes and she
shook her head rapidly. But Mashell's mind was already
made up. The two teens would *never* guess they were
listening to their conversation. They'd just be two girls
gathering their school supplies, getting ready to go home.

They walked into the building as quickly as they could,
keeping their faces turned from the Blade's view. This was
no time to draw attention to themselves. Anna had the sense
to wait until they were inside the school before she made
the gesture of the cross—fingers to her forehead then her
chest then from shoulder to shoulder—and whispered
fervent prayers in Spanish.

Mashell paused in front of the classroom door and
whispered, "Don't worry girlfriend. How they gonna
know we listenin'? We'll act like we packin' up our stuff
to go home."

"But what if they recognize *me* as Ricardo and Luis' *sister?*"

Oh. Mashell hadn't thought of that. "Then we just can't let 'em see us."

She scanned the hallway, made sure it was deserted and entered the room. It was a math class, with posters praising algebra and geometry on its bland, beige walls. Swishes and thuds and the metallic thumps of a trash can being dumped carried through a door that opened to the next classroom. The school janitors were hustling through their daily chores.

This room still had pencil stubs and paper wads scattered on the carpeting. Which meant they hadn't cleaned it yet. Maybe they'd be in here any minute. Or maybe they'd start running a vacuum cleaner and she wouldn't hear a word the teens said. There was no time to lose.

She hurried to the desk nearest the window, quietly set her books on it, and dropped to her knees. Anna did the same. It was *vital* they keep themselves from being seen through the window, and Mashell told her friend so in an urgent whisper. Not that Anna couldn't have figured that out for herself . . . .

Mashell shimmied to the edge of the sill and rose up on her knees until her upper body was straight. She cocked her ear toward the opening—and could barely make out what the older teen was saying in a hushed voice.

"Hey, man, what you worried about? That *posse* of theirs is *nothing* compared to us. We'll squash them, you know? Like cockroaches."

The younger teen didn't sound convinced. "But what if they get me first?"

Disdain entered the Blade's voice. "You *afraid,* man?"

"No," said the kid in a voice that sounded just the opposite.

There was a long silence and the sharp smell of smoke drifted in through the window. The Blade must have lit a cigarette. His voice was even harder as he remarked, "If you weren't my cousin, the Blades wouldn't look twice at you."

She heard leaves and branches rustling. The older teen must be leaving. At the same time, a husky man's voice thundered behind her. *"What you girls doin' at that window?"*

"Window!" the Blade yelled. "Somebody *heard* us?"

The two girls whirled and stared in startled fright at a
burly janitor with streaks of gray in his black hair. "You got
no business bein' here," the man went on. "You just get
yourselves on home or I'll write a note for your teachers."

The janitor's threats were the least of Mashell's worries.
Heavy footsteps pounded past the window, heading toward
the main entrance. The Blade was coming in here, after
them! "We gotta get *away!*" she told Anna in a quivering
voice. Thank goodness the janitor wasn't blocking the
door! Moving quickly into the main hallway, they ran as
fast as their legs could move—away from the front door.

But their footsteps echoed off the tile, calling as loudly
as a trumpet for their chasers to follow them. Mashell
skidded around a corner, then jerked Anna to a stop long
enough to hear the teens' footsteps pounding behind them.

The girls had no choice but to keep running and pray for
a hiding place.

6

"Girls' bathroom!" gasped Anna as they raced down a third hallway.

"No—good! He'd—trap us in there! You think—he gonna obey—the rules an' stay out just 'cause he—a *guy?"* Mashell's words came out in clusters as she panted for air. She nerved herself to glance over her shoulder. The Blade was still out of sight.

Don't let 'im see us, God! Please don't let 'im see us! She was as horrified at the thought of him discovering who they were as she was of him catching them. And he was gaining on them. She was almost certain she could hear his footsteps right behind hers and Anna's.

If only they could find a girl's restroom that had a door on each end and a large crowd of young ladies in it that they could blend into! Anna must have been thinking along the

same lines. *"The girls' locker room!"* she continued.
"They're holding—tryouts for the seventh-grade track—
team today! We could join them!"

But then she gave a frustrated groan. "It's on the other
side—of the school, though!"

Mashell fought down panic. They'd have to double
back somehow, without running straight into the Blade.
Anna suddenly surged ahead, yanked open the right side of
a set of double doors and beckoned her friend to go in.
Mashell shot past her and stood with trembling muscles,
staring at a large room with rows of long tables. The
cafeteria, of course.

The only light came from long windows in the wall
alongside the outside eating court. It was dim in here
compared to the bright hallways with their fluorescent
lights. And totally quiet. But this was no time to gaze at
surroundings. Anna was already tearing toward the
cafeteria's far door.

The girls reached it together and shoved both sides
open—into the face of the younger, wannabe Blade! He
gave a cry and grabbed his nose. Anna screamed.

Mashell surged past them both. "Come *on!*" she yelled.
She needn't have bothered. Anna was shoulder to shoulder
with her in seconds. Then ahead. They'd nearly reached the
end of the hallway when the cafeteria doors burst open and hit
the wannabe again, this time on the shoulder. He bellowed in
pain once more as his older partner pushed past him.

"Get outta the *way!*" roared the Blade. "Why didn't you
grab one of 'em?" The girls had rounded the corner and
were out of earshot before the younger teen could answer.
Anna angled them toward a large blue door near the
hallway's end, on the left. Mashell could see letters etched
in white on a strip of black plastic near the top of the door.
She hoped with all her heart they said . . .

Girl's locker room! Yes! They stumbled through it, then
through the next door at the end of a short entryway that
opened to the locker room itself. With hot relief, Mashell
took in the jabbering, constantly-moving pack of girls that
lined the benches, changing from street clothes to school T-
shirts and shorts. A few girls gave them cool, uninterested
glances. Mashell was happy to be ignored, now.

She beckoned Anna to an empty space on a middle
bench. Her friend sat beside her, looking like she

felt stupid and out of place, too. And still scared. Mashell
bent over and untied her tennis shoe, just for something to do.

The Blade *had* to know they were in here! Maybe he was
in that little entryway right now. Maybe he'd peek through
the door. She braced herself—her muscles already felt as tight
as guitar strings—waiting for it to open a tiny crack. And she
willed herself not to look, not even to sit up. She gave Anna's
ankle a warning squeeze and she bent and fiddled with her
laces too.

The only door that opened was the one to the coach's office.
A tall, thin woman, with legs as lean and muscle-lined as an
Olympic runner's, walked rapidly into the changing area. She
was dressed in the same T-shirt and shorts as the girls, only
she had a silver whistle around her neck. She wore her hair
pulled back in a tight knot—a lot like Mashell's, she was
pleased to see. And her *eyes!* Long-lashed with rich brown
pupils. She could have been the queen of an African nation.

A beautiful lady. But an intimidating one.

She surveyed the group; most of them had finished
changing. Mashell moved closer to Anna. They were the
only two still wearing street clothes, and she felt like a
giraffe at a dog show. "Most of you are ready, I see," the

coach said, eyeing the two misfits. "I'm glad a good number of you are trying out. If you don't have your gym outfit with you today—"(she gave Anna and Mashell another glance)—"I have some spares in my office. Follow me and I'll get you lined up. The rest of you, *head out*. My assistant is waiting on the field. She'll warm you up. Let's *go*, women!"

She clapped her hands and the other girls hustled out the locker room's other door. Mashell caught a glimpse of concrete and green grass and peach-colored benches before it shut.

It was beginning to dawn on her how perfect this situation was. They were about to change into clothes that neither the Blade nor the wannabe would recognize. They'd blend into a crowd of girls trying out for—what team was this again? She hoped it was something she was halfway good at. She wasn't in the mood for total humiliation.

The coach pulled two sets of brand new shorts and shirts out of a trunk in her office that was piled full of them. "Either buy 'em or get 'em back to me clean by the end of the week," she told them. "And I suppose you haven't filled out your health forms yet."

Before they could even give each other confused
glances, she handed them yellow papers full of questions
like "Do you bleed easily?" and "Have you ever been
hospitalized?" There was also a space for a doctor to sign.

The coach wrote their names on a clipboard she was
carrying, then told them to hurry as she walked rapidly
toward the outside door. Anna made sure they were alone
before she blurted out, "I gotta get *home!* Mama's gonna be
worried sick!"

Mashell winced. Something *else* she hadn't thought about!
"So's my grandma," she moaned. "I'll prob'ly catch it *big
time* when I finally show up. I'll get grounded 'til I graduate."

"Shouldn't we leave now?"

"The Blade and his buddy might be watchin' for us. We
gotta give 'em plenty of time to search. Then they'll just
give it up an' go away." Mashell stared at the hallway door;
the Blade might be waiting behind it this very minute! She
lowered her voice. "I don't *care* if I get in trouble! We
gotta get home *safe!*"

Anna bit her lip. "But we've got to warn Ricardo and
Luis! Did you hear what they said? That the Blades are
going to crush their posse like *cockroaches?*"

"We gotta change clothes, anyway. You *know* they watchin' the hallway door. An the field too, prob'ly."

Anna reluctantly agreed. She even remembered to change her hair. She'd worn it around her shoulders all day, with just a little of it pulled back; now she yanked it all into a high ponytail that fanned down from the top of her head. Mashell hid her own purple hair wrap in her pocket and let her braid hang down instead of keeping it twisted in a tight knot.

Anything to make themselves look different, in case the Blade caught a glimpse of them.

Three red-faced, panting girls trotted inside to use the bathroom as the coach hollered "Hustle *up!*" through the door. Anna and Mashell went outside with them and immediately joined in the warmup exercises as though they knew what they were doing. Mashell kept her eyes riveted on the assistant teacher, hoping she didn't look as clumsy as she felt.

She tried desperately to follow everyone else's movements, but her body wouldn't cooperate. Or maybe it was her mind that was confused. When the group swung its legs left, she kicked right. By the time she corrected the movement, they were kicking the *other* way. Her arms circled forward when theirs went backward. She bent over as they straightened up.

Maddening. Embarrassing. But worst of all, attention-getting. She noticed smirks on the faces of girls around her, which was bad enough. But what if the *Blade* was watching her? The assistant coach let them flop on the grass for a rest and she scanned the streets around them as subtly as she could. No sign of him or the wannabe. Maybe they'd left. Or maybe they were watching from a hiding place.

The coach had the girls form a line. "We're going to time you," she told them, "starting with the fifty-yard dash. One girl at a time, run from the white line here to the one my assistant is standing beside. Now, notice the stop watch in her hand. She'll set it, then she'll tell you, 'Ready . . . *go.*' Take off just as *fast* as you can and keep going *all out,* top speed, until you cross the other line and get completely past her. Any questions?"

Mashell couldn't keep a grin off her face. She was going to *like* this! She'd always been a fast runner, and she was especially good at bursts of speed over short distances—from home plate to first base during a fistball game, for example. She'd never been a strong hitter, but she ran so fast she usually got the infield players flustered enough to fumble the ball. Or maybe they didn't realize they needed to throw hard toward first base. Either way, she almost always beat the throw.

She watched, fascinated, as the first few girls ran the fifty yards between the lines. Most of them made the mistake of slowing to stop before they passed the assistant—and got yelled at for it. "Keep going! Keep going! Remember we're *timing* you!" bellowed the coach. "Slow down *after* you cross the line!"

Mashell was next. She wasn't *about* to make the same mistake. She placed one foot in front of the other, hunched down a little and set her gaze on the far white line. The assistant had her thumb poised to push the watch's start button. "Re-e-a-a-d-y-y-y," she yelled, drawing out the word. Mashell took a deep breath.

"Go!"

She lunged off her front leg and tore toward the line as though the Blade was hot on her heels. Her feet thudded on the concrete so hard and so rapidly that the world—except for the line—turned into a jarring blur. The girl grunted

through her teeth as she crossed it, but didn't let herself
slow down until she was completely off the concrete, with
her feet swishing through short grass.

Her body trembled and her lungs heaved, but she was
too excited to feel really tired. She became aware of claps
and cheers from the watching girls. And the coach
shouting, "That's it! That's how to do it! Did you see how
she burned the track up? She came out *smokin'* and didn't
slow down, either!"

The uncontrollable grin popped back out on Mashell's
face. "Best time so far!" shouted the assistant teacher.
Anna beamed at her.

Not everyone showed such pleasure at her performance,
though. A cluster of four seventh-grade girls stood glaring
at her through narrowed eyes. "Don't you live at Gordon
Brown?" one of them asked.

Uh-oh.

The girl went on without an answer. "Yeah, you do! An'
none of us remember seein' you in our classes. In fact, we
don't think you go to school here! You only in *sixth grade!*"

She sounded like she was accusing her of murdering
somebody. Mashell had no idea what to say, so she stood in

silence, fighting not to stare at Anna in desperation. No
sense in embarrassing *her,* too.

"What's this?" asked the coach, striding up to them.
The woman listened to the girls' accusations with one
eyebrow curved up. Mashell stayed quiet. Her face was
throbbing with heat, and not just from running.

The coach showed a kind heart underneath her stern
outer image. She brought Mashell into her office so
she could confess the truth in private. Anna very gallantly
went along.

"We had to get away from that Blade!" Mashell told her.
"Hidin' in the locker room was all we could think of! See,
he didn't get a good look at us, so we figured we could get
lost in the first crowd we saw."

The coach shook her head. "Why in the world did you
risk listening in on a conversation between two gang
members?"

Mashell chose her words carefully. She wasn't going to
lie, but she couldn't tell *too much* of the truth, either. "When
we was outside the school buildin'—when the older Blade
first showed up—we overheard 'em say somethin' about
Anna's brothers. We afraid the Blades are out to *get* 'em."

She didn't say why.

"Do your parents know where you are?"

"No!" said Anna. "My mama will be really worried. I was supposed to be home an hour ago!"

The coach offered to call them. When she learned that neither girl's family had a telephone, she called a community volunteer at Gordon Brown, who promised to deliver her message to them. "Tell their parents I'll give the girls a ride home as soon as my team tryouts are over." she told the worker.

Both girls thanked her, which brought a smile to the coach's face—and made her even more beautiful. She looked at Anna. "Would you like to *really* try out for the track team, as long as you're here?"

Anna shrugged and gave a self-conscious giggle.

"Couldn't hurt to try," the coach urged her again. Then she fixed her eyes on Mashell. "*You* can thank me by promising me you'll try out next year. You're a good runner."

The girl grinned from one ear to the other. "I promise!"

* * * * * * * *

An hour later, Mashell and Anna were dressed in
their regular clothes again—a blouse and a jeans skirt
for Anna and a sleeveless pullover and leggings for
Mashell. The coach led them across the school parking
lot at a brisk walk. "Did you get everything?" she
asked them over her shoulder.

Mashell suddenly felt uncomfortable. Were they
forgetting something? Why did it feel funny to have
empty arms? Oh! "Our books!" she blurted out. "We
musta left 'em in the math room!"

The coach drove them around to the school's main
entrance, then waited in her car while the girls ran
inside. The books were right where they'd left them, on
the desk next to the window. But they were scattered
all over the top of it. A few papers and Anna's science
textbook had fallen to the floor.

Mashell frowned. "Didn't we leave 'em in two
stacks? We musta bumped 'em when we ran by—"

Her speculations were cut short by a horrified cry
from Anna. Someone—the Blade, obviously—had
scrawled her brothers' names in black letters across the
front of her three-ring binder. And a line was slashed

through each name. It was the Blade's way of saying
that he knew exactly who'd listened in on his conversation. The slashes through Ricardo and Luis' names
meant he and his gang were out to kill them.

Anna covered her face and burst into tears. And
once again, Mashell had no idea what to say.

Carlos saw a small crowd of children clustered at the grassy end of the Gordon Brown parking lot. Their parents weren't letting them play in the neighborhood park for awhile, because of the drive-by shooting. So they gathered close to home. The lot wasn't as big as the park's playing diamond, and the ball sometimes rolled out into the street, but it was better than doing nothing.

Carlos' team, the Good News Club, gave a cheer as he and Felipe (and Peppy, trotting beside him on his leash) walked up to them. Which only made Carlos feel worse. They were counting on him to be their home-run hitter, and he knew he could have come through for them, in spite of his bandaged knees and elbows. Felipe could've run the bases for him.

But he couldn't play for a completely different reason, as he tried to explain to his team. (They were gathered around Peppy, patting the dog's neck and stroking his back while he sat on his haunches and looked delighted.) "It's my stupid sister. She didn't come home from school, and Mama says I gotta look 'til I find her. Anybody seen her or Mashell around?"

No one had. "Girls! They're probably sitting on some bench gabbing about clothes!" His voice went high-pitched as he imitated them: "Oh, sorry, Carlos! We were so busy talking we *completely* forgot about the time!"

He sounded angrier than he really was because under his mask of disgust he was worried for the girls' safety. What if they were missing because the Blades . . . .

He couldn't stand to finish the thought.

The boy heard footsteps behind him and a voice that made his knees and elbows tingle, and put him in a worse mood than he was in already. "Should we finish the game we started the other day, or beat these guys from scratch?" said Jose.

The other team cheered and laughed. Carlos glowered at him and Tamyra, who were busy slapping their hands together. "The only way you can beat anybody is by cheating! I'm *glad* I can't play today if *you're* going to be in the game!"

Jose gave Carlos a fierce glare before he fired back an insult peppered with swear words.

"*Ooooh!*" said the kids.

Carlos was mad enough to start a fist fight. But he checked himself. His first order of business was to find his sister. He could take care of a foul-mouthed cheater later. And he told him so.

Jose shouted another insult at him as he left, of course. Which would have ruined his already dark day, but a movement behind him made him pause and look. Felipe trotted up beside him. "I'll help you look for the girls," he said. "We can play fistball some other time."

Suddenly Carlos' afternoon seemed brighter.

* * * * * * * *

The sun was low in the sky, and its rays gave every wall and pole and tree trunk an amber glow. The boys' shadows stretched as long as skinny giants' and Peppy's looked like a grizzly bear on stilts. And they still had seen no sign of the girls. They ran into some members of Ricardo and Luis' posse at the park. The teens didn't know where the girls were either, and they promised to join the search if they didn't show up by nightfall.

The two boys and the dog wound up trudging toward Carlos' house, discussing what they should say to Mama, when a brand-new, burgundy-colored car pulled up alongside them.

The door opened and Anna's voice stopped them in their tracks and drew a bright *yip* of greeting from Peppy. *"Carlos!* The Blades are out to get Ricky and Luis! We gotta *warn* them!" She and Mashell scrambled out of the car onto the sidewalk beside them.

Carlos was too surprised (and relieved) to comprehend what she'd just babbled. *"Where were you?* And whose *car—"*

He froze as one of the most beautiful women he'd ever seen pulled herself out of the driver's seat and leaned against the roof to speak to him. "My name is Ms. Monroe. I'm driving your sister and her friend home for their safety."

"You're the phys ed teacher at Douglass!" cut in Felipe with an awe-filled voice.

"That's right."

Anna was nearly dancing with impatience. *"Please,* Carlos! We gotta warn Ricky and Luis *right now!"*

"You need to go home, right now!" said Ms. Monroe, firmly. "Talk to your parents first, *then* do whatever warning you need to do. Or better yet, let them take control of the situation."

No one said anything for several tense seconds. The only noise was Anna's sniffling. For the first time, Carlos noticed her red eyes and wet cheeks. Ms. Monroe went on. "Is this your neighborhood?"

The kids nodded.

"Point to your house."

"The white one down there on the corner, with the dark green trim," answered Carlos obediently.

The coach waved the girls back into her car. Mashell opened the door on her side, reached in and gave something to Anna, who held it up for the boys to see. It was her three-ring binder. At the sight of his brothers' names in black, with slashes through them, Carlos' face went pale and he had to fight to breathe. *"Who put that on there?"*

"The Blade who chased Mashell and me all over Douglass! If we hadn't ducked in the girls' locker room, he would've grabbed us." Fresh tears spilled out of Anna's eyes. *"Now* do you see why we've gotta warn Ricky and Luis right away?"

Prickles ran up and down Carlos' arms and legs and neck and back. He could hardly speak above a whisper. "Their posse's at the park. I bet Ricky and Luis will go there to meet them right after they finish work." He glanced at the sky. "Which is right about *now.*"

A sob escaped Anna. "Get in the car, girls," ordered Ms. Monroe. They did what she said. "Do you want a ride too, boys?"

"Uh, no thank you," answered Carlos slowly. "We've gotta go—take care of something."

Anna stared at him through the car's rear window as it pulled away. Her eyes were full of worry mixed with hope. He waved at her, then broke into a fast run,with Felipe and Peppy racing along beside him.

They reached the park as the sun began to set, spreading a rose-orange glow as bright as fire across the parts of the

sky they could see through the building-cluttered horizon.
Moms and grandmas tugged their children away from the
swing sets, in a hurry to get them safely home before dark.
Someone drove by with a stereo thumping out a rock bass
pattern and a rapper shouting in rhythm.

He and Felipe scanned the park for any sign of the
posse. Had they left? Gone to someone's house? They'd
be safe inside. Carlos wished he knew where they were so
he could relax.

Then Felipe caught sight of them, leaning against the
outside wall of the public bathroom. The waning light made
them show up as little more than black silhouettes. They
were laughing and joking as they always did. Maybe they
had given up plans to venge Rudy. All Carlos knew was
they had to break apart and get home *now*.

The two boys and the dog had hardly stopped running
since they'd turned away from Ms. Monroe's car. Carlos
paused long enough to catch his breath. His lungs and
throat were burning, probably from breathing heavily in the
smoggy air. He bent over and rested his hands on his knees
just long enough to feel his heart begin to slow.

He hoped his brothers' posse would listen. It occurred to him that he hadn't prepared anything to say. Should he tell them about Anna getting chased by a Blade? That would only make them angry, wouldn't it? Then they'd go out *looking* for members of the street gang!

He'd tell them about the slashes through their names, anyway. And warn them to get away from L.A. for a while. The sooner the better. He straightened up, beckoned Felipe to follow and loped toward the teens.

It didn't take them long to notice the boys. "Here comes the world-famous fistball player!" said Luis with concern in his voice. "What are you two guys doing out here this late, man? And don't tell me Mama let you either, 'cause I'll know for sure you're lying."

Carlos poured out his warning. The teens' faces grew hard and somebody—Ricardo, maybe—swore. "If the Blades think we're gonna run away like scared rabbits, they got another thing coming," Luis declared. "We'll get them before they get us!"

"I don't think so," yelled a voice in the dark. Three gunshots exploded nearby, like minibombs. Carlos felt a shock on his right leg, as though someone had touched a hot

electric wire to it. And suddenly Carlos' thigh had no
strength. He instinctively shifted his weight to his left leg
and stared at his right. He was horrified to see dark liquid
soaking through his jeans.

"*CARLOS!*" cried Luis with a break in his voice. "He's
been *hit!*"

And now his thigh started to throb and throb and *throb.*
He couldn't help but start to cry. He could feel the warm
liquid (he knew what it was, now) streaming down his leg.
His heart began to pound and his head felt like it was
spinning in circles. *I've been shot! I've been shot! Am I
gonna die?*

The boy was vaguely aware of strong arms wrapping
around him and bringing him gently to a lying down
position. Only he didn't feel grass under him. He was
resting across someone's lap. The world went dark. He
heard Peppy yelping frantically and a babble of frightened
voices shouting things like "*No,* not Carlos!" and "We gotta
get an *ambulance!*" and "He'll bleed to death!"

He forced his eyes to flick open (when had he closed
them?) and saw Luis' face close to his. Luis' eyes were wet

and he was murmuring, "Lord Jesus, don't let my little brother die! Please! I'll do anything!"

And then the pain became so intense that it seemed to roar in Carlos' ears. He couldn't hear anything over his own cries. Everything faded away except the agonizing, aching pulses in his thigh. And then they faded away too.

8

Carlos felt his body moving, though he wasn't doing anything himself. His arms were rising and so were his chest and head . . . and legs. That vicious throbbing started in again. And then he was aware of arms underneath him. Someone was lifting him. Or rather, two people were.

"It *hurts!*" he whimpered.

"Be *careful* with him, you guys!" said someone sharply. Carlos knew that voice. Ricardo's.

The arms set him down on something soft. His body rocked gently as the arms withdrew. Hands tucked a blanket over him and fastened straps around him. His head came to rest on a pillow and he opened his eyes to a Los Angeles night sky, with the few stars that showed made so dim by street lights and smog that they looked like pin holes. Not that he cared in the least.

If only these men (whoever they were) would make the pain go away! He started to cry, softly. One of them leaned over him, with his face upside down to Carlos'. "We may need to give him some painkiller. Poor little guy isn't very comfortable."

"I'll ask the doctor," said the other. Carlos vaguely heard a hissing, thin-sounding voice coming from a two-way radio. The ambulance driver was asking questions like, "Okay, what dosage?" Then he knelt beside him. "Carlos, we're going to tilt you toward the right. Hang in there, all right? I'm going to make the pain go away."

Both men gently turned him on his right side. (He couldn't help but cry out at the pain shooting through his leg.) The driver rubbed something cool and wet on the backside of the boy's hip (where were his jeans?) that made his skin tingle as it dried. Oh no! That could only mean one thing.

"Are you gonna give me a shot?" Carlos asked in a voice that begged the man not to.

The driver patted his shoulder. "You'll be trading a big ache for a little sting. Once this stuff takes effect, your leg won't hurt anymore."

The sting wasn't so little, though to his relief it only lasted a moment. Then both men settled him on his back again and standing at each end, picked up the thing he was lying on. It jerked and swayed as they carried it.

Ricardo and Luis and Felipe walked alongside, looking frantic with worry. Ricardo held Peppy's leash and snapped *"No!"* at him as the retriever strained to reach his young master. The two teens noticed Carlos looking at them, and Luis found his hand under the blankets and clasped it. "Hey, Champion, you're gonna be okay! We'll get you back playing fistball in no time. How 'bout it?"

"Okay," murmured Carlos. Luis let go and the boy reached his shaking hand toward Peppy. Ricardo let the dog surge in close and Carlos scratched his ears and smiled a little as Peppy licked his arm.

"Don't worry, pal, your boy here is gonna be fine," the driver told Peppy. He gave Ricardo a look that caused him to jerk Peppy sideways, out of the way. The men set the stretcher down, opened two huge, hinged doors in the back of the ambulance and lifted him into what looked at first like a square, black hole. It was the inside of the ambulance, of course—dimly lit. He was beginning to feel sleepy. Tingling numbness was slowly taking over his whole body until he realized he didn't feel the ache in his thigh anymore.

Carlos heard something humming softly beside him, but raising his head and looking around at the metal boxes and instruments took too much effort. He was perfectly happy looking at the milky white ceiling, until even that became too hard to concentrate on. He closed his eyes.

"I think he's had enough pain killer," said one of the men. His voice sounded far away and muffled. The vehicle lurched as the back doors slammed shut. The boy was barely aware of Peppy's faint, high-pitched barks that quickly faded as the ambulance started moving. Carlos was asleep before he had time to feel sorry for his pet.

* * * * * * * *

Two people were lifting him again. He opened his eyes, not to a low ambulance ceiling but to white tiles high overhead and long, narrow rectangles of painfully bright, fluorescent light. Carlos was settled on another soft thing that was higher off the ground than the stretcher had been. A bed maybe, with long metal bars running along each side. He was wrapped in a blanket again, and the rest of his clothes were gone, replaced by something that felt like a giant paper towel.

Another upside-down face—a lady's, this time—smiled at him. (She looked strange. She had on a baggy green smock and trousers and a puffy paper cap on her head, like she was going to take a shower, fully dressed. He almost giggled.)

"Hi." she said. "You're awake. Do you feel any pain?"

He wasn't sure *what* he felt, so he shook his head. More people (dressed like the nurse) came alongside the bed. The lights started to move. No, *he* was moving. He was being rolled down a hallway.

His leg was starting to hurt again. *Really* hurt. And why was his left arm smarting? The boy turned his head to look and was shocked to see a thin metal tube taped to the underside of his forearm and jabbing deeply into it. It was attached to a tiny, transparent hose that curved down from a bottle with clear fluid in it. The bottle hung from a pole that

someone was pushing right along with him. Which meant it
was on wheels too.

I-V tube, short for *intravenous*. Now, how did he know
that? He had a sudden image of a homeless old man he'd
met several months ago. Clarence. That's right! He'd
come to visit Clarence in the hospital after he'd been beaten
by a street gang. The old man had an I-V in his arm, keeping him alive. Carlos winced as he remembered hoping
he'd never get one stuck in *him*.

And here it was. Funny, but it didn't hurt as much as he
thought it would. He suddenly wished he could see somebody he knew. Was he alone? Did anybody besides God
know where he was? He wanted his *family*. His throat
suddenly tightened and he struggled to keep from
whimpering out loud.

"Where's my mom and dad?" he asked the nearest face,
a young man. "And my brothers and sisters?"

The man looked helplessly at the nurse, who explained,
"They're right here in the hospital, waiting in one of the
lounges. They can't be with you this moment because you're in
a section of the hospital where visitors aren't allowed. But they
are here. So don't worry, Carlos. You're not alone. Okay?"

How did she know what was bothering him? The bed
turned a corner. Then its pushers guided it through a pair of
sliding doors that said NO ADMITTANCE in large red letters.

More white ceiling. More white lights. Lots of metal
boxes with dials and blinking lights. And a long tray on
wheels, as tall as his bed, covered with things that made his
heart race and his palms grow wet. Pointed things. Sharp
things. Needles.

Two other nurses lifted him one more time, to a long,
flat, padded thing that looked like a cross between a bed and
a table. The head nurse walked around until her face was
finally right side up. She was smiling again. "Carlos,
you're about to undergo surgery."

Surgery! Were they going to cut him *open?*

Her voice became even more soothing. "You don't need
to worry about anything. That man beside you is going to
put something called *anesthesia* in your I-V. It'll put you to
sleep. You won't feel any part of the operation at all."

The man gave him a grin and shook his free hand.
"How's it going, Carlos? My name's Mike. Like the lady
said, you won't even know what's happening 'til you wake
up and it's over."

What if I never wake up? thought Carlos. He was too frightened to speak. Mike must have seen the fear in his eyes because his smile faded and he spoke in a low voice, obviously trying to keep the boy from hearing him. It didn't work. "I'd like to get the creeps who shot this kid in here for an operation. I'd give them only enough anesthesia to keep them under for *half* of it."

The nurse gave him a look that was part scolding, part agreement. Then she and Mike and the other two nurses bustled around Carlos, talking about things he didn't understand at all. He wished they'd get too busy to notice him, so he could climb off the table and sneak away.

But they were busy about *him*. Wiping his leg with more of that quick-drying stuff. Putting more scary-looking things on the tray. Checking the machines.

His heart was thumping harder and harder. He was beginning to shiver and it took all the fight in him not to scream and cry. Then Mike said, "You're going to sleep now, Carlos. Your arm will feel cold and then you'll be under. You're doing a great job, sport!"

The young man was certainly right about the cold. Carlos' forearm suddenly felt like Mike had sent ice water into its veins. And then his head, his whole body, felt heavy and muffled, as though someone had wrapped him in an invisible lead blanket. He seemed to sink under the weight. He had no choice but to shut his eyes. Everything went silent. His thoughts stopped.

And in the very next instant he was struggling to open his eyes again. The invisible blanket was still around him, but it was growing lighter. His whole body felt fuzzy and the table seemed to be rotating slowly. Or, wait...he wasn't on the table anymore. He was back on that bed with the metal sides.

When were they going to start the operation? Carlos wished they'd get it over with! He struggled to raise his head but his neck was too floppy to cooperate. "He's waking up," somebody said. The voice seemed right in his ear and far away at the same time. A nurse whose face he hadn't seen before leaned over him. (She wasn't wearing a shower cap like the others. She had short, curly, brown hair.) "How are you feeling?"

"Dizzy." His voice came out in a rasping croak and his words were slurred. "Aren't they—going to—operate?"

She grinned. "They did already. You're all through, and now you're in the recovery room. The doctor said it went well, and your leg should heal completely."

No way! They couldn't have done the surgery in one second, which felt like the amount of time he was asleep.

No way! She seemed to guess his thoughts. "I'd let you see the stitches, but they've put you in a cast. See?"

The nurse raised his blankets enough for him to stare in bleary surprise at his right leg completely wrapped in a sky-blue, fiberglass cast that was bent slightly at his knee. Now that he was thinking about it, his leg felt heavy. It started to hurt too, but with a different kind of pain—a steady ache instead of throbs that burned. Relief warmed him all over. The surgery was over, and he was okay!

The nurse gave him a sip of water, which tasted *wonderful*. And made his voice work, too. He had dozens of questions. "What's making that beeping noise?" . . . "Which machine tells you my heart is working?" . . . "How long will I have to lie here?"

She hadn't answered nearly enough of them before she had to hurry to another patient. He was left to his own curiosity as he took in his surroundings: a long room with colorful, happy things on the walls—balloons, teddy bears, kittens, puppies. And lots of beds like his, half surrounded by floor-to-ceiling curtains, some empty and some with sleeping or restless children on them.

All the kids had wires running from their bodies to machines on wheeled carts. Carlos did too. He peeked under his paper smock at something that looked like a round Band-Aid stuck on him, with a wire attached to it. The wire sent his body's life signs to the machine.

He'd heard the sound it made before—pa-*tap,* pa-*tap,* pa-*tap,* like water drops hitting the plastic lid of an empty coffee can. Clarence had been hooked to a monitor, too. Carlos felt amazed. The taps were the rhythm of his own heartbeat.

The I-V was still in his arm. It didn't hurt anymore, but it was starting to *itch.* He didn't dare touch it. It stung a little every time he moved, and he could just imagine how much it would hurt to scratch it. He lay back and listened to the murmuring voices and whimpering kids and clicking footsteps and bleeping machines. He was starting to feel bored and wished he could see his family. But he felt excited and happy, too. He'd made it through surgery! His leg was going to be fine.

He was still alive.

9

Carlos had never felt so cared for, so important, so *fussed* over in his life. Doctors walked into his hospital room and asked him questions and shook his hand and raved about how brave he was. Nurses helped him hobble to the bathroom and taught him to swing himself down the hallways on crutches. They brought pills and pillows and meals on a tray. They pushed buttons that caused half his bed to rise like the back of a recliner rocker.

He had his own little table that reached across his bed or rolled out of his way. (Everything seemed to be on wheels around there.) The food was good—Rice Krispies cereal for breakfast and macaroni and cheese for lunch and a hamburger and french fries for supper. Every meal had juice and milk with it, and fresh fruit or carrot sticks.

And dessert! Vanilla pudding and a brownie for lunch
and strawberry ice cream for supper. Everything came
wrapped in plastic or covered with a metal lid. Too bad he
couldn't unwrap his food at home! It was a little like
opening birthday presents.

He had lots to look at—wallpaper with rainbows on it,
as many books as he wanted to read and his very own
television screen, hanging at an angle from the ceiling. But
his favorite things were the gifts he'd gotten: a brain-teaser
puzzle, an airplane model kit and red carnations in a pot
shaped like a football. And cards! At least a dozen of them,
from small notes to a poster-sized one made by his fifth-
grade class at Fern Street Elementary.

Luis gave Carlos a new nickname that everyone else
picked up on: Champion. He and Ricardo gave him a card,
just from the two of them. And they and their friends in the
posse pitched in and bought him a new soccer ball. "To
play fistball with, of course," they said.

He wasn't alone, either. He had a roommate—a
talkative boy named Antonio—who had been in a car
accident and had both legs and one arm in casts. Carlos'
own injuries suddenly didn't seem so bad.

Mama and Papa and Anna and his brothers—together or
by themselves and in every combination in between—
stayed by his bed and talked to him or to each other or read
or watched television. Only one thing took Carlos'
cheerfulness down a notch: the hate-filled anger that every
so often filled Luis' eyes. He looked more determined than
ever to seek revenge against the Blades. But Anna
whispered something to Carlos that took away *some* of his
worry, anyway. (They were alone for a few minutes while
Papa went to get a cup of coffee and Antonio was asleep.)

"Ricky and Luis can't venge you, yet. No one in their
posse can. They don't know for sure who shot you. Or
Rudy, either."

Carlos frowned. "But you know, don't you? You
overheard the Blade and the wannabe talking about it."

She squared her shoulders stubbornly. "Maybe I did.
But *I'm* not about to let them know it. There's been *enough*
shooting around here!"

Good going, Anna! He grinned at her. Ricardo and Luis
and their friends couldn't very well seek revenge against
someone if they didn't know who did the wrong. He hoped
they'd *never* find out.

The next day he had a big surprise. He'd just awakened
from an afternoon nap and was about to start flipping
television channels when the door to his room opened and a
crowd of children and adults surged into the room and
surrounded his bed. The Good News Club!

Felipe gave him "thumbs up." Mrs. Peterson and Mrs.
Joyce planted kisses on his cheek. (Right in front of
everybody!) Maria and Victoria, bumping shoulders as they
carried it by the string, presented a gigantic tinfoil balloon
to him. On one side it showed Superman's red "S" with the
words "Get well, hero!" printed over it. On the back, the
club teachers and kids had written their names in black
magic marker.

He flushed red and felt like his grin was going to split
his face. Everybody clapped. Then the teachers shooed the
club out of the room. Mrs. Peterson (with a nurse
supervising) helped him out of bed, into a bathrobe and
down the hall to the lounge where the others were waiting.
He was lowered into a wheelchair while Miss Lindstrom
took her guitar out of its case and led them in singing.

Soon the room filled with curious adults and other
young patients wearing casts or neck braces or bandages.

Many of them, including Antonio, rode in wheelchairs.
Carlos was glad he could walk on crutches part of the time,
anyway.

Mrs. Joyce introduced the onlookers to the Good News
Club and led them all in reciting a Bible verse in a chanting,
rap-like rhythm until they knew it by heart. Mrs. Peterson
told the Bible story, continuing the one she'd started
last meeting.

"The club kids were introduced to these twin brothers,
Jacob and Esau," she said, pointing to the paper figures on
her flannelboard. She quickly reviewed the story for the
benefit of the newcomers and ended with, "Esau wound up
hating Jacob. Does anyone remember why?"

Mashell raised her hand. "Because Jacob was a cheater!
He swindled Esau out of the money and power he was
supposed to get as the oldest brother."

The older, middle-aged lady nodded and went on with
more questions. But Carlos didn't pay much attention. His
thoughts went back to that day on the playground when Jose
tripped him just to win a round of wallball. Hot anger hit
him and he found himself in complete sympathy with Esau.
He would have hated Jacob too. As far as he was
concerned, cheating was unforgivable.

Mrs. Peterson said something that drew his attention back to the bright-walled lounge now crammed with a sprinkling of adults and many children, sitting on the two stuffed couches or on folding chairs or in wheelchairs. "Well, Jacob the cheater wound up *getting* treated the way he treated his brother. He lived with and worked for someone who cheated *him* even worse."

Carlos listened with interest as she told how Jacob ran away from his home to escape Esau, who still wanted to kill him. Jacob traveled hundreds of miles to the home of his uncle Laban. Laban had two grown-up daughters, and Jacob fell in love with the younger one named Rachel. He wanted to marry her, and Laban said yes. But then Laban disguised his older daughter, Leah, and made her marry Jacob instead! Jacob didn't realize he had the wrong wife until it was too late!

He angrily asked his uncle why he'd done such a thing and Laban answered, "It's not our custom around here to let the younger daughter get married before the older one does. So, you take Leah as your wife and then I'll let you have Rachel too." (Laws back then allowed men to have more than one wife.)

But Laban added a huge "oh-by-the-way" clause to his deal. He told Jacob, "I'll let you have Rachel if you work for me for seven years."

Seven years! Jacob was upset and angry. But he loved Rachel so much he gave in to his uncle's unfair terms. The young cheater, now being cheated by his uncle, worked as Laban's sheep and goatherder. He fed the animals and took care of them when they got hurt or sick, protected them from predators and made sure they had healthy babies.

Finally his seven years of labor were over and he married Rachel. But Laban conned him into working for him *another* seven years! And then he tried to cheat Jacob out of the sheep and goats he had earned through all his hard work. But God was with Jacob and saw to it that he had large herds of animals to take with him back home.

Leah and Rachel had given birth to children too. At last, after over twenty years, Jacob packed up all his belongings, put his wives and children on camels and began the long journey back to his father Isaac's country.

"And who do you suppose he met on the way?" Mrs. Peterson asked the group.

"Esau?" guessed Felipe.

Carlos leaned forward a little, hanging on every word she said. *Did Esau still want revenge? And was he going to get it?*

"Jacob had a *big* problem!" she explained. "Here he was, with thousands of sheep and goats and donkeys milling around and his wives with children—some of them only babies—sitting helpless on camels. Jacob had a few servants to help him, but not nearly enough men to fight a battle. And he'd received word that Esau had *four hundred men* traveling to meet him. That could only mean that Esau was out to wage war against him. He and his wives and children would be slaughtered!"

She paused. "Do you think Jacob was scared?"

Everyone nodded.

"You're right. He was *petrified.* He begged God to help him. He picked out hundreds of his best animals and had his servants bring them to Esau as gifts. He knew he deserved to die for the way he'd cheated his brother. Do *you* think he deserved to?"

"Yes!" blurted out Carlos. "Esau was finally going to get his revenge!"

Even before he'd finished his sentence, he was struck by the awful thing he'd just said. Wasn't this how Luis felt?

But Carlos realized he didn't want Jacob to die any more than he wanted Luis to kill the guy who shot him. Vengeance was no solution. Not even against kids who cheated to win wallball games.

Mrs. Peterson must have seen the turmoil on his face. She let silence settle over the lounge and stood looking at him with one eyebrow raised, waiting for him to voice his feelings. He finally mumbled, "I didn't mean that. Revenge ain't any good for *anybody.* Too much killing's going on."

He gave Anna a quick glance. Her eyes were brimming with tears.

"Good, Carlos," said Mrs. Peterson softly. She raised her voice to "teacher volume" again. "I'll go on with the story. It could have ended horribly, with Esau and his men sweeping down on Jacob's people with spears and swords. Innocent men and women *and children* would have been killed. But this isn't a sad story that teaches us a sober lesson. It's a joyful one. Why, do you suppose?"

Anna blurted out, "Because Esau forgave Jacob?"

"That's right. He met his younger brother face to face, threw his arms around his neck and kissed him! And they both cried for happiness."

The entire room broke into applause. Carlos shut his
eyes and pictured his brothers grasping arms with the
Blades, not for a fight, but in friendship. No more
vengeance. No more violence.

Mrs. Peterson went on to tell the group that Jesus taught
His followers to forgive too. He acted out His own words
by asking God His Father to forgive the Roman soldiers
who pounded spikes in His wrists and feet and left Him
dangling on the cross! Then she asked if any children
wanted to pray to ask Jesus to be their Savior.

Several hands went up. Carlos listened while they
repeated the words he had said himself not very long ago. A
prayer telling Jesus that they believed in Him, that they
knew He died for them to take away the punishment they
deserved for the wrongs they'd done. Words of gratitude.
Words of worship, that declared Jesus was no longer dead
but alive forever. Words of joy, knowing that because they
asked, He'd let them live forever with Him.

Carlos felt warm inside. He glanced at his right leg,
wrapped in stiff blue fiberglass and resting across another
chair that someone had set in front of his wheelchair. He
added his own silent prayers as Mrs. Peterson finished her

spoken one. *Lord, I forgive the guy who shot me. Will You help Ricardo and Luis to forgive him too? And as soon as I get back to running, I'm gonna play fistball. And Jose's gonna be the first person I ask to play.*

Anna was hurriedly wiping wetness from her eyes. She smiled, but he could still see worry in her eyes. And a stab of it hit him too. What if his brothers refused to forgive? What if they found out who shot him? Terrible images came into his mind.

He couldn't make them go away. He could only keep praying.

10

Mashell loped onto Frederick Douglass' school grounds, hoping she hadn't missed Anna. Oh good. There was still a large crowd of teens milling around, jumping onto bikes, walking past her with those cold looks she was learning to steel herself to.

It was a relief to see Anna. The same three friends walked with her. "Someone in my phys ed class told me *you* tried out for the seventh-grade track team," one of the girls said to Mashell. "Is that *true?*"

Mashell rolled her eyes and nodded and her face grew warm. "Long story."

The others pressed her for details, but she changed the subject. They left for home without knowing any more than they'd heard from rumors. Mashell wondered nervously what *else* the teens at Frederick Douglass were saying about her.

But she'd have to worry about that later. She had
something more pressing to deal with at the moment.
"Anna, you got a school yearbook?"

"Yeah. It's at home."

"How 'bout we look at it? The wannabe Blade goes to
school here. Maybe we can spot his picture and learn his
name. An' then we'll have a better idea who the homeboy
was, 'cause he called the wannabe his cousin."

Anna winced. "Do you think that's a good idea?"

"Couldn't hurt! I'm really curious! Ain't you?"

Anna cocked her head. "Yeah, I might as well admit
that I am. But, you won't tell anybody, will you? If
Ricardo or Luis find out . . . ."

"No way, girlfriend! The shooter's name won't even
cross my lips! I promise!"

They decided to rush straight to Anna's bedroom as
soon as they made sure Felipe could escort Maria and
Victoria and Loeesha home. He wasn't thrilled with the
idea, and the three little girls wanted to tag along with "the
big girls," of course. But Anna was firm with them for
once. "Mashell and I have something important we need to

do by ourselves. We're going to run all the way, and you'd never keep up. You'll see us soon. Don't worry."

Then they turned and loped away before Maria or Victoria or Loeesha (or Felipe) could raise more protests. They hurried along, mixing walking with jogging, until Mashell's heart thumped against her ribs and her lungs hurt as though she'd inhaled most of L.A.'s smog.

They stumbled in the Hernandez' front door, and the first thing Mashell noticed was a delicious smell: cinnamon and something wonderful deep-frying. Carlos was sitting at the kitchen table with his leg stretched out on a chair. Peppy lay beside him with his tail thumping the floor and a look of ecstasy on his face. It was obvious how he felt about having his young master home.

Both girls greeted Carlos. "How you doin'?" Mashell asked him.

He grinned at her. "Great! Mama made a treat just to celebrate me coming home from the hospital!"

He seemed about to explain what it was, but Anna had grabbed baby Rosa and was whirling her around at arms' length. The toddler and the teen giggled and squealed loudly enough to drown out conversation. Mama smiled and out of politeness forced herself to speak English. "You got a friend today, Anna?"

"*Si,*—uh, yes." Anna caught herself. She was obviously used to speaking to her mother in Spanish. She quickly added, "The others will be along in a little while. Mashell and I have something we want to do."

Mama looked confused and Anna translated what she'd just said.

"*Buenas tardes (*good afternoon, pronounced boo-AY-nahs TAHR-dace), Mrs. Hernandez," said Mashell, proud that she'd gotten the phrase right. Anna had been teaching her bits of Spanish, so she knew *tardes* was the proper afternoon greeting. *Buenos dias (*good day, pronounced boo-AY- noce DEE-ahs) was used in the morning.

Mama grinned at her. "*Buenas tardes!*" She was busy rolling a ball of dough into a fat rod about eight inches long. Then she took a fork and pressed grooves in it until it looked like it was covered with lengthwise stripes. She waved her fork toward the table. "Sit down and have some *churros!*" *(*a dessert pastry made of deep fried dough, pronounced CHOO-roce, with the "r" flipped.)

Carlos was already eating a batch that Mama had deep-fried. They were rolled in a mix of *azucar y canela* (sugar and cinnamon, pronounced ah-SOO-kahr ee kah-NAY-lah). Mashell had eaten churros at Mexican restaurants and she *loved* them. Who *cared* about wannabe Blades in school yearbooks?

But Anna remembered their task. "Can we take them to the bedroom on a plate?" she asked Mama in Spanish. "We'll be careful to clean up the crumbs." Mashell guessed what she was saying by her gestures and she hoped Mama would say yes. They hadn't run all this way to waste their time snacking. They needed to be in the girls' room *alone.*

Mama *did* give in. Mashell started to grab a plate stacked with warm, puffy, cinnamon-smelling rods. Then she hesitated and caught Anna's eye with a silent question. Should they invite Carlos to come with them? He'd certainly be interested. After all, they were trying to figure out who shot him!

Anna shook her head so subtly that only Mashell could see the gesture, and that was because she was looking hard at her. She was right. He'd just gotten home from the hospital. He didn't need to know who nearly killed him. Not yet. Maybe not ever.

Anna apologized to him for leaving him alone and promised him Felipe would be along any minute. "Good! Sitting around the house all day is *bor*—ing!" he exclaimed. Then he shot a glance at Mama and whispered, "But what are you two going to do that's so *top secret?*"

Mashell raised one eyebrow. *"Girl* stuff!"

"Anna's got a *crush* on some guy, right?" asked Carlos with a sly smile.

"Never you mind!" Mashell hurried toward the girls' room, wincing at the teasing remarks he sent after her and Anna. She hadn't actually *spoken* a lie. But wasn't it dishonest to make Carlos *think* they were doing something different than they actually were?

She'd have to worry about feeling guilty later. Rosa toddled after them but Mama tugged her back to the kitchen. The baby girl gave an indignant wail or two, but a churro dangled in front of her face quieted her in an instant. Mashell's last glimpse of her before Anna shut the bedroom door was of a pudgy toddler with wide dark eyes and black ringlets framing her face, stuffing her mouth full, with cinnamon and sugar specks covering her cheeks and fist and arm and shirt . . . .

Mashell snatched up a pastry and took a giant bite. She had to quit chewing long enough to gasp and *mmnh* in delight. Crisp and sweet and tangy with cinnamon on the outside, flaky and just a little chewy on the inside. *"Ooh, girl,* your mom can cook!" she raved. Anna nodded. She was too busy eating to answer. But before she'd finished chewing her first churro, she wiped the sugar off her fingers and pawed through a pile of books in her corner.

Mashell couldn't get over how cramped the room was, with three twin beds pushed against three walls and two beat-up dressers on either side of the closet. A small square of bare wood floor showed in the middle. The floor space around the dressers was covered with shoes and crayon boxes and tiny balls and puzzle pieces. And two dirty, ragged-looking dolls.

Its walls were painted pale yellow-green (*disgusting color,* she thought) and it was peeling in places. Anna had taped a few posters over her bed. Maria and Victoria had put up pictures they'd colored. There were no bedspreads, only blankets and pillows. But the room was neat. And Mashell had nothing to feel smug about. She had to share her room with Loeesha, and they didn't even have a dresser. She kept her clothes in boxes in her closet.

Anna found what she was looking for and the two girls sat cross-legged on the floor with their backs against a bed, bent over the class book and munching churros. "I'll look through your class first," Mashell mumbled, scanning the rows of tiny black-and-white photos on each page. She wished her eyes were camera lenses so she could just blink and keep the image of each face clearly in her head.

No wannabe, yet. Anna suddenly clapped both hands down on a page with a tiny gasp and a giggle. "Come on now, lemme see you!" Mashell coaxed her.

Anna rolled her eyes. "It's an ugly picture! I look like a pocket gopher!"

"Girlfriend, you couldn't look ugly if they caught you first thing after you got outta bed!"

Anna giggled harder and shook her head firmly. But Mashell refused to give up until her friend's hands finally slipped away from the picture. She peered closely at it. "Oh, that ain't bad at all!" she said in a scolding voice. "You lookin' *good.*"

But Anna remained unconvinced. "My cheeks are swollen. Like I've got the mumps."

"What we *doin'?*" Mashell suddenly squeaked. "We got *work* to do!"

And they were running out of time to do it. A commotion in the rest of the house made both girls stiffen. The others were home! They could hear young voices babbling in excitement about something. The churros, no doubt. Mashell frantically flipped through to the eighth-grade pictures.

"I hope the girls eat slowly, 'cause they'll want to play dolls in here when they're finished with their snack," murmured Anna.

Mashell reached the ninth graders and her eyes seemed drawn to one photo like a pin to a magnet. *"Hold on!"* she hissed. "I think I see 'im! Fourth picture, third row down, left page. Among the "D's." She placed her finger under it and Anna bent to look while Mashell found the name. "Julio Diaz" (pronounced HOO-lee-oh DEE-ahz).

Anna suddenly looked pale. "Please don't tell *anybody* you found out his name! Not Carlos or Felipe or *anybody.* If this gets back to Ricardo and Luis, they'll go after *him* for shooting Rudy and his older cousin for shooting Carlos! And maybe they'll get killed trying! Or they'll kill this boy and then the police—"

Her sentence was cut off as the bedroom door slammed open. Luis surged into the room, his eyes filled with rage.

"Did you say *Julio Diaz* shot Rudy? *Did* you?"

Both girls sat speechless. He snatched the book from the floor in front of Mashell and scanned the pages until he found the young teen's picture. "Yeah. Yeah. That's him. Diaz. We thought so!"

His eyes narrowed. "That means his cousin is the *asesino* who shot Carlos!" He tossed the book on Anna's bed. "And I swear it's the last thing he'll ever do!" He ran from the bedroom, his footsteps pounding through the house. The front door banged open and shut. He was gone.

The two girls stared at each other in blank horror. Until Anna could recover enough to do two things—scream Luis' name and burst into tears.

They heard the rocking clump-*clumps* of Carlos, hurrying down the hall on crutches. He leaned against the doorway and stared at them with terror on his face. "What *happened?* Luis ran outta here like the house was on fire! And he looked mad enough to—to kill somebody."

"Oh, *Carlos!*" wailed Anna. "He overheard us talking about the kid who shot Rudy. And now he knows who shot *you!*"

The boy looked horrified. "Why did you *lie* to me? Why did you make me think you were looking at future *boyfriends?* Why didn't you tell me what you were *really* doing?"

"We—we didn't want you to find out—" mumbled Mashell.

He cut her off, in a voice that was getting louder and higher by the second. "Luis was here all the time, helping Papa in the backyard! He came inside for a snack and I sent him to *spy* on you! I thought he'd overhear you talking about some guy Anna had a *crush* on! I thought it would be *funny*—"

His voice broke. He was obviously too upset, and too scared, to go on.

"I—I didn't mean to lie," said Mashell in a pleading voice. "The *last* thing I wanted was for your brothers to find out—"

Her words faltered and she stopped trying to explain herself. Anna was crying too hard to hear her. And nothing she could say would help.

11

Mashell was as angry with herself as she had ever been. *Girl, here you go again, stickin' your nose in somebody else's business! Why you have to be so curious? If Luis gets himself killed or shoots somebody else ....*

He *couldn't!* He just couldn't! She rose to her feet. *I gotta do somethin' 'bout this!*

Carlos was sitting on Anna's bed, looking numb. Anna was still crying softly. They both glanced at her. "I'm goin' after 'im," she told them. "I'm gonna talk Luis outta doin' somethin' stupid."

The glaze instantly left Carlos' eyes. "But you *can't!* You could get shot *yourself!*"

"Too bad! If it hadn't been for me, he never woulda learned the name of the Blade that shot you. I ain't just

gonna *sit around* waitin' to hear he been shot—or arrested
for killin' somebody else."

Anna snatched a tissue from a box beside her bed. "No,
Mashell! You aren't to blame! Didn't you
hear Luis? He was already pretty sure that Julio Diaz
shot Rudy."

"And it was my stupid idea to have Luis listen in on
you," added Carlos.

Mashell was too furious at herself to be deterred. "No,
it was *my* idea to look up Diaz's name in the first place. So,
I'm gonna *do* somethin' about it!"

She stormed from the room. Once she left the
Hernandez house, she had no idea what she'd do next.
Where could Luis be? How would she find him? *I'll walk
all over Watts if I got to!*

She passed through the front of the house with a rapid
"Thank you" to Mrs. Hernandez, who was busy frying
another batch of churros. The woman nodded and waved.
Mashell remembered to catch the screen door before it
slammed and began walking blindly in the only direction
she could think of—toward the park.

Creaks and clump-*clumps* and fast footsteps behind her checked her stride. Anna ran up beside her. "I'm going with you!"

"So am I!" snapped Carlos.

"You can't, Carlos," argued Mashell. "You'll hurt yourself worse. Ain't you supposed to stay quiet?"

"No! The doctor says if I don't get exercise my leg'll get weak—"

"But he didn't mean you should go all over the city!" Mashell pointed toward the house. "Go on back home! You'll just slow us down. You want us to get to Luis too *late?*"

She had him, and she could tell he knew it. He opened his mouth to argue, but there was nothing he could say. He brought his right crutch down with a *crunch* on an empty soda pop can lying on the sidewalk. Then without a word, he turned and lurched toward the house.

"What'd you tell your mom?" Mashell asked Anna.

"That I wanted to spend some time with you. I left before she could ask when I'd be back." Anna sighed and looked back at the house. "I hope it won't be too late. Mama trusts me, and I don't want to disappoint her. She's been through enough worry."

"Well then, let's get goin'!" Mashell broke into a trot, fighting away the little voice inside that urged her to ask her own mom and grandma for permission to go to the park. After all, what if they said no?

* * * * * * * *

There was no sign of Luis or the rest of the posse. Not in the park. Not anywhere around Gordon Brown. Not near Frederick Douglass. They decided to try the high school next, but that was many blocks away and the sun was nearing the horizon.

Mashell was ready to give up. Maybe Ricardo and Luis and their friends had already carried out their vengeance. The thought made her shudder. These boys weren't *evil!* They loved fun and they cared about their families and they worked hard and they weren't mean. What kind of a world turned them into killers?

She was about to suggest they turn around and head for home when she heard a young man's voice shouting their names. Anna brightened up for the first time since they'd left her bedroom. *"Ricardo!"*

The Hernandez' dingy orange pickup truck pulled up beside them, looking more wonderful to Mashell than a brand-new Cadillac. "Get in," he told them in a voice they didn't dare disobey. "Carlos told me what you're up to. Do you know how *stupid* it is for you to be wandering around right now? The Blades know we're out for revenge. What do you think they'll do to *you?*"

"You ain't gonna drop us off at home, are you?" asked Mashell in a small voice.

"I should. But we're too far away and I can't take the time. I think every second counts if I'm gonna find Luis and get him home safe." He gave them a sharp glance. "Now that I finally found *you!*"

Hope rose in Mashell like a firecracker. "You mean, you givin' up the venge?"

"I want to get my hotheaded brother off the streets 'til he calms down."

Mashell hopped in beside Anna. It was all she could do to keep from squealing with excitement.

"You girls have to promise me something," he went on, firmly. "And I mean *promise.* Like, your most solemn vow. Understand?"

"Depends on what it is!" said Mashell, surprised she had the cheek to answer him, especially after the tone he'd used.

He glared at her. "Promise me you'll stay in this truck no matter what. You won't get out for *any reason.* And if I tell you to duck you'll do it in a *millisecond.* Okay? You *promise?"*

They promised. Then they rode along in silence. Ricardo was definitely not in a talkative mood. He kept muttering things in Spanish that made Anna cringe. Mashell was dying to know what he said, but she wasn't about to ask her friend to translate.

She was *starving,* too. It was past supper time, by now. The sun had nearly set and there was no sign of Luis. He wasn't at any of his friends' houses.

"Is Luis *loco?"* (crazy, pronounced LOH-koh) Ricardo raved as they pulled into another friend's driveway. "Does he think he can take on the Blades *alone?"*

He slammed the driver's door shut and loped to the front door of the fifth house they'd visited. He stood on the porch and carried on a loud conversation with his friend. Ricardo was getting more and more agitated. Mashell could see fear growing in him. It was growing in her too.

She glanced out the rear window and saw something that made her heart stop for one terrified moment. A brown Chevy Camaro—the car that the drive-by shooter had been riding in! She screamed Ricardo's name and he looked wildly toward the street.

"Duck, girls!" he bellowed. He and his friend dropped to their stomachs as gun shots burst from the car. Mashell pushed Anna to the truck floor and flopped over her with her arms wrapped around her own head and shoulders. Which meant she heard the faster-than-lightning *crack* of the rear window shattering and the bullet slamming into the truck ceiling, instead of seeing it.

Her own screams drowned out every other sound after that. Until Ricardo yanked open the driver's door and poured out frenzied questions. "Are you all *right?* Mashell? *Anna!"* Ricardo pulled his sister out of the truck and into his arms. "I should have brought you home!" he rasped. "You girls could have been killed!"

Anna didn't answer him. She rested her head limply on his shoulder, and if she hadn't kept her legs straight, Mashell would have thought she'd fainted.

Her eyes fell on the gaping hole in the back window, with straight-lined cracks fanning out from it like a web made by a robot spider. A wave of nausea welled up and she scrambled outside and made a beeline for the nearest bush.

She was quivering so hard she wondered if she was going to collapse. But she didn't throw up, anyway. Suddenly strong hands clutched her shoulders and guided her back to the pickup. Ricardo jumped in, hardly bothering to brush away the tiny cubes of safety glass that covered the seat. "I'm taking you home! Luis is going to have to take care of himself!"

"We'll look for him," his friend assured him. "Don't worry. I'll get our posse together and we won't rest 'til we find him."

With enemies like this after Luis, Mashell couldn't bear to think what shape he'd be in when the posse found him. If they found him.

* * * * * * * *

Carlos could hardly stand to go to bed. There had been no word from anyone about Luis. Mama and Papa, after chewing out Anna and Ricardo at the top of their lungs, hugged them and cried. Anna's eyes were nearly swollen shut from all the tears she'd shed by the time the evening was over.

Papa went to a neighbor who had a telephone and called the police. Two officers arrived and questioned Anna and Ricardo. And left shaking their heads. "We'll keep up a close watch for him," they said. But Carlos could tell they didn't feel much hope.

He didn't have much to hold on to, either. Why had *no one* seen his brother? He poured out prayer after prayer for Luis' safety.

Carlos went through his usual routine of face-washing and teeth-brushing, disgusted that he had to balance on one leg. His crutches slipped away from the corner he'd propped them in and clattered to the floor, and he nearly fell trying to pick them up. He wanted to throw them through the window. The boy might have tried it if Mama hadn't hurried into the bathroom to help him change into pajamas and half-carry him to bed. Her eyes were nearly as red as Anna's.

Carlos didn't even have patience for Peppy, who begged him to wrestle and didn't understand why his master couldn't. He shoved his dog away from him and yelled, *"No!* Go bug somebody else!"

He felt instantly sorry. But Peppy didn't seem to have hurt feelings. He simply stretched out on the floor beside Carlos' bed and watched his master with smiling eyes. The boy almost resented him for it. Why couldn't *he* be a dog, whose only concerns were food and play and sleep? Why did he have to be a human, who looked at his brother's empty side of the bed with sick dread in his stomach?

It felt as though the lights had only been out for a few minutes when someone rapped loudly on the door. Carlos sat straight up. Ricardo switched on a lamp as Papa hurried to answered it. Anna and Mama followed at his heels. Maria and Victoria and Rosa were obviously asleep.

It was a police officer. A different one than the two who had stood in the doorway earlier in the evening. His face was sober and he kept clearing his throat. The fact that he had Mama sit down made Carlos' heart pound so hard that it thumped in his ears.

He shut his eyes and wanted to cover his ears so he wouldn't hear the awful words the officer quietly said. "Mr. and Mrs. Hernandez, it's my sad duty to inform you that we found your son lying behind a Dumpster, in an alley along 103rd Street. We rushed him to the hospital, where he was pronounced dead on arrival from a single bullet wound to his head."

Mama crumpled into Papa's arms. Anna threw herself into Ricardo's, who lifted her over to Carlos so he could sit on the bed and hold them together. Anna and Mama sobbed and sobbed and sobbed. But Carlos could hardly hear them. He was crying too hard himself.

12

They kept Luis' casket closed, "because of the nature of his wound," they said. Which only made Carlos angry. That couldn't be Luis in there! It *couldn't!*

He wished it wasn't, with a longing deeper than anything he'd ever felt. He imagined how good it would feel if Luis strolled into the living room, cracking jokes the way he always had. He found himself imagining it was all a mistake. Luis was fine! He was just lost! The boy would nearly get himself to believe it, and tiny splashes of joy would land on his heart like raindrops on a desert. But then reality would burn them away like the blazing sun on a black rock.

He yearned to go back to the time when his brother was alive. *Why isn't he alive? I want him to be alive!*

He hated having to sit all dressed up at the funeral home as sympathetic people squeezed his hand and murmured kind words that meant nothing to him. *They* didn't know how much it hurt to lose Luis! A few old ladies even had the gall to pat his cast. He wanted to snarl, "Get your hands off and leave me *alone!*"

The boy took a pin to his "Get well, hero!" balloon. The explosion it made as the point burst its skin felt good, somehow. It instantly shrank and sagged and flopped to the floor. *I ain't no hero! It's my stupid joke on my sister that caused Luis to find out who shot me. If I hadn't sent him to listen in on her and Mashell* .... He nearly stuck himself with the pin, and called himself a coward for not doing it.

He *hated* the person who shot Luis. He hated the person who shot *him.* And he was angry with the girls. *If they hadn't lied, and made me believe they were gonna talk about boyfriends* ....

He didn't want to visit with anyone. Not his Good News Club teachers, not Felipe, and especially not Mashell. They tried to talk to him, but he turned them off with a few sharp words. "I'm okay. Really, I am. I just wanna be left alone."

Nothing could make him feel better, not even Peppy's affection. In fact, the dog's constant begging for attention

only irritated him. Carlos asked Papa to leave him tied up
in the backyard and his plaintive whines and yelps didn't
even phase him.

He wanted to hide where no one would find him again.
And instead, the next day, he had to join his family, walking
slowly down the aisle of a church with everybody staring at
him. He had to sit through the funeral with droning organ
music and some lady singing songs he didn't know or like.
His whole family was crying around him. Even Papa and
Ricardo wiped tears. But he didn't. He couldn't. The boy
felt too dry inside to cry.

*God, I prayed for You to save my brother! Why didn't
You? Don't You love him? Don't You love my family?
Didn't You hear me? Why did You let him die?*

He decided he'd never pray for anything again. God
didn't listen to him, so why bother? The priest was saying
something about Jesus saving mankind from punishment
forever. And to add to his hurt and his anger, Carlos
suddenly felt fear. *What if Luis wasn't a Christian?* He
began to tremble, and a few cold tears finally came. *What if
his brother wasn't in Heaven?*

The boy lifted up a rapid prayer, out of sheer habit. *God, Luis is there, isn't he? Please let me know!*

He stopped himself. *No more praying, remember?* It seemed as though Jesus didn't want to hear from him, anyway.

* * * * * * * *

Mashell had felt guilty before, but never like this. She could tell Carlos was angry with her and she didn't blame him. It was *her* fault Luis was dead.

Grandma had grounded her for staying out late and wandering around Watts without permission (as if she would have gotten it) and nearly getting herself killed. *And my help made such a difference!* she told herself bitterly. *If it hadn't been for me, Luis would still be alive!*

All she could do was lie across her bed, and draw pictures on scrap paper with a stumpy pencil, and read the same magazine a dozen times (she didn't have anything else to read), and snap at Loeesha when she came in the room.

Until the police officer showed up at her door. "Your name is Mashell, right?" she asked. She had a trim build and wore her black hair pulled back in a tight knot. A pretty lady. But there was a strength behind her eyes that convinced Mashell she could stand up to any criminal out there.

"My name is Lucy Garcia and I'm here to ask you some questions. Don't be scared 'cause I'm a cop. You're not in trouble, okay? I just wanna know about the drive-by the other night. Pretty scary, huh?"

Mashell rolled her eyes. "Yeah! Thought I was gonna die."

They sat in the living room, on the sagging, frayed couch with olive-green flowers on it (Mashell had always hated that color). The policewoman pulled a small notebook and pen out of her shirt pocket. "Can you describe the car?"

Perfectly. And she did so without hesitation. Officer Garcia wanted to know if she'd seen anyone's face. "Not this time," Mashell answered, and went on to describe how Ricardo and Luis's friend Rudy got shot by the wannabe Blade from the same car. She told about overhearing the young teen talking to his homeboy cousin, the older Blade who'd chased her and Anna into the girls' locker room.

Garcia took rapid notes and listened with intense
interest. And kept interrupting her with questions. Then
she said, "Well, your story matches your friend Anna's
perfectly. Thanks for your help." She continued to smile,
but sternness entered her eyes and Mashell knew she was
about to be scolded.

"Next time, leave the gangs to us, okay? You try to be a
hero and you'll wind up like Luis. That sounds pretty harsh,
but it's true, you know?"

Mashell nodded and glanced at her lap. "I know."

"Listen to Grandma. Stay safe at home. You're too
pretty to get messed up with the gangs. You got too much
to live for. Okay?" She rose to her feet and grasped
Mashell's hand while the girl chuckled and mumbled,
"Okay." (Her face felt hot.)

Grandma ordered her back to her room and she paced
the floor, bursting with curiosity, overflowing with
unanswered questions. Had the police found the bullet
jammed in the ceiling of the Hernandez's truck? Would
they find the gun it had been shot from? Did they have any
idea who killed Luis? Would they arrest Julio Diaz, the
wannabe Blade who shot Rudy?

She stared restlessly at her room's scuffed, off-white walls. She'd put up a few pictures of her favorite singers, but one of them kept falling down and Grandma said they were out of tape. Her eyes shifted to the gray floor tiles with some squares missing. The room's only furniture was the bed and a kitchen chair covered with cracked vinyl that she used as a bed stand. What a place to be grounded in! It was *ugly* in here!

Loeesha's toys were scattered all over the floor—mostly little things like yo-yos and single crayons and spoons from a doll dish set. In a burst of disgusted energy, Mashell scooped and kicked and tossed them into a jumbled pile in the corner.

And went back to stewing over the questions that bothered her most. Were Ricardo and his posse still bent on revenge? When was the violence going to end?

Lord, don't let nobody else die around here. 'Specially not Ricardo. I don't think his family could take it.

The next day she saw something that only made her more worried as she walked from school with Felipe and Loeesha. (Carlos and Anna and Maria and Victoria were still in mourning and wouldn't return to school for at least

another week.) She caught a glimpse of three teens from
the posse, standing together on a street corner. They were
wearing oversized, floppy shirts, perfect for hiding
weapons under.

She watched them head toward the park. Their eyes
were hard and they were almost marching, like soldiers on
their way to a battle.

Felipe saw them too. "They look like they're ready to
kill somebody," he whispered in her ear.

Mashell nodded. She felt sick. "You think they gonna
get in a fight?"

"I dunno. All I know is, I ain't gonna be anywhere
around. I'm going *home!*" Felipe quickened his pace and
Mashell sped up too, until Loeesha (who had no idea what
was going on) had to run to keep up, complaining all the
way.

The memory of the bullet smashing the truck's rear
window rang through Mashell's mind. She didn't want to
be around any more shooting, either. She hurried alongside
Felipe, feeling like a refugee in a war zone.

He ran into his living unit with a goodbye wave.
Mashell made Loeesha keep hustling. Only one more block

to home and safety. Why did she feel so afraid, anyway?
She wasn't fighting in any gang war. But she couldn't
shake the intense feeling that she needed to get *home.*

As she passed the trash Dumpster on the corner, she
heard a sharp, scared-sounding whisper. "Hey, *you.* Stop a
second. Please?"

She jumped and stared in shock. *Who's that?* Loeesha
hadn't noticed her sister stop. She skipped to their unit's
front door, pulled it open and disappeared inside. Thank
goodness she was safe, anyway. Mashell was torn between
curiosity and a desire to run for that door as fast as her legs
could carry her.

She was beginning to think she was hearing things.
Until someone crawled from behind the garbage bin and
knelt beside it, keeping one shoulder pressed against it and
looking around him like a terrified fox being hunted by a
pack of hounds. He was the last person Mashell ever
expected to see.

The wannabe Blade. The young teen who'd shot Rudy.

"What do you *want?*" Mashell demanded, keeping all her muscles tense and ready to run.

"Keep your voice down! Speak soft! I don't want nobody to know I'm here!" Diaz stared around, making sure no one was watching them. She'd never seen so much fear in anyone's eyes before.

He began to explain himself, at last. "You're Anna Hernandez' friend, 'cause I saw you running through the school with her when my cousin was chasing you."

"What about it?"

"You gotta do something for me. You gotta tell your friend's brothers to get outta town or they're gonna die. The Blades are out to get them."

She snorted in disgust. "Why don't you tell me somethin' I don't already know? Didn't you hear 'bout Luis Hernandez? He *dead!*"

Diaz shut his eyes in a grimace as though she had caused him physical pain. His voice sounded shaky. "I didn't *know.* I've been hiding. The police are after me. So are the Blades. Even my cousin. They're calling me a traitor 'cause I don't wanna join 'em anymore. But I'm *sick* of all the killing! I didn't wanna shoot that guy! They made me! They would have beat me *up* if I hadn't."

He set his eyes on Mashell, but she could tell he wasn't really seeing her. "I keep picturing him lying on the sidewalk. I didn't wanna *do* it!"

A noise behind them made him hunker down. His desperate eyes never stopped looking around.

"Just a cat," said Mashell.

He blew out air with a sharp puff. "I'm getting away from here. I'm gonna get myself a new life some place else. I got relatives in New Mexico . . . ."

His voice trailed away and she saw him relax a little. But only for a moment. He rose on his knees and said, "You gotta stop the posse before they get in a fight with the

Blades. I seen 'em gathering at the park. They got guns and knives and everything. But tell 'em to *drop* it, you know? To get away from here. I know my cousin and the other Blades. If they think somebody's out to get 'em, they'll attack *first*. And they outnumber the posse, prob'ly three to one."

His words made Mashell want to turn on her heels and run toward the Hernandez home, as fast as she could. Maybe Ricardo was there. Maybe she could give the warning to him, and then he'd talk his friends into giving up the fight. There wasn't a moment to lose.

But something made her stay put. The young teen's body was trembling from the fear he carried. She felt sorry for him. And amazed at the risk he'd taken. "Thanks for the warnin'," she murmured. "You ain't no coward. An' you ain't no traitor. You tryin' to save somebody's life."

He stared at her in surprise. She was glad he didn't try to answer, because she had something else to say. She poured the words out rapidly, before embarrassment could swallow them. "I'm gonna pray you get to New Mexico safe. An' you know what else? Jesus loves you. Even when you do somethin' awful. I did somethin' I coulda gone to jail for. An' I told 'im I was sorry. He forgave me, an' He'll forgive you too."

Her body flushed with warmth.

"Thanks," he muttered. Her words had put something in his eyes, under the fear and despair. Hope, maybe? He suddenly bolted from the Dumpster to the palm tree on the corner. Then from there to some crates beside a wire mesh fence. Then she lost sight of him.

As if she had time to stand around staring. The posse needed to hear the warning, before they started a war with the Blades that one way or other, they'd lose. She started to run toward the park. Then she remembered Grandma and the grounding she'd just gotten free of. She raced home.

Mom met her at the front door, looking disgusted. "Why didn't you come home right away with Loeesha? You gettin' on my *nerves,* girl!"

"I stopped to talk with a—friend."

She went on quickly, before Mom could ask her to explain. "Can I go over to Anna's? She needs somebody to make her feel better." Mom could hardly argue with that. She'd been to Luis' funeral with Mashell. She'd seen the girl sobbing in her papa's arms. Thank goodness Grandma wasn't within earshot. Mom let her go.

She raced toward the Hernandez house as fast as her legs would move. She hadn't lied either, Mashell told herself. She really *did* want to comfort Anna. After she made sure Ricardo was properly warned.

* * * * * * * *

Carlos sat sideways on the living room couch, disgusted with its lumpy cushions and his sore bottom and his itchy leg. He wanted to break his cast into pieces so he could get at his thigh and scratch it. He wanted to break the television set too. There was nothing on except soap operas and news shows and baby stuff. He'd die before he'd watch *Barney* the dinosaur.

His eyes fell on the bed—his own, now—and his bad mood got worse. The boy could hardly stand to sleep on it anymore. He remembered wishing he didn't have to put up with Luis' snores. And elbows in his face. And blanket-

hogging. And practical jokes, like the time his teen brother
put earthworms on his pillow.

But last night, he would have given anything to feel the
bed sag under his brother's weight. Tears ran sideways
along his face and trickled into his ears and dripped onto his
pillow. Maybe he'd ask Mama if he could sleep on the
couch tonight.

Someone was knocking on the front door. *Drat!* Mama
was in the backyard, hand-washing clothes in the square steel
tub. Anna was in her room, probably crying again. Maria
and Victoria were outside, playing with their stupid dolls.

He'd have to answer. "Who *is* it?" he bellowed, the way
Mama had taught him.

"Mashell," a familiar voice hollered back.

He gave an angry grunt. What did *she* want? He
wanted to tell her to go away. Instead he yelled,
"Come *in.*"

She looked agitated. "Hi, Carlos. Ricardo here?"

"Why do you wanna know?"

She poured out a rapid explanation, something about running
into the kid who shot Rudy and about the Blades looking for
Ricardo's (and Luis') posse. She ended with a frantic plea.

"I gotta find Ricardo. I gotta warn 'im! The posse can't fight the Blades! They can't! The killin's gotta *stop!*"

Carlos gave an angry grunt. "Why should it? Why shouldn't Ricardo venge Luis? *Why shouldn't the guy who killed my brother die?*"

She stared at him with shock and disbelief on her face. "But—Carlos," she stammered. "You—you always—" She pursed her lips. "What about forgiveness? You know, like Jacob and Esau—"

"That's just a stupid story! This is real life!"

"It from the *Bible!*"

"Who *cares!* I don't believe in God no more. He didn't answer my prayers. He didn't keep my brother alive. And now, for all I know, Luis is lost forever. Where the devil is."

Her eyes narrowed in alarm. "You don't know that! You couldn't read Luis' mind! Maybe he believed in Jesus!"

Carlos shrugged.

"I bet he did! But anyway, *you* gotta keep believin'! You *know* Jesus loves you. He *died* for you, didn't He?"

Carlos wanted to fling his crutches at her. "Why don't you leave me alone! Leave *all* of us alone! If you had told me the truth instead of telling me you and Anna were gonna look at *boyfriend* pictures, I wouldn't have sent Luis to spy on you! He wouldn't have found out who shot Rudy! *Maybe he'd still be alive!*"

The shock on her face was instantly replaced by hurt. Her lips quivered and she spoke softly. "I—I told you I was sorry. I never meant no harm. I'd give anything to have Luis still alive. I'm—*sorry!*"

He turned his face toward the couch so she wouldn't see the huge, hot tears that burned his cheeks like acid. He heard her turn and run. As the door slammed behind her, he thought he heard her crying too. And he was glad.

* * * * * * * *

The afternoon dragged into early evening. Mama came inside and started chopping tomatoes for supper. She said nothing to him. She hardly spoke at all, lately.

There was another knock at the door. *It better not be Mashell again!* Mama opened the door and Carlos gave the visitor a surprised glare. *Mrs. Peterson! What is she doing here?*

She was carrying her briefcase. She grasped Mama's hand and said, "I have something important to show you. May I come inside? I'll only take a moment."

The woman was carrying food with her too, in plastic grocery bags. Carlos caught glimpses of rice bags and tomato cans and cereal and powdered milk in boxes. Mrs. Peterson carried them to the kitchen and set them on the floor beside the refrigerator. Mama dabbed her eyes with a tissue and whispered, *"Muchas gracias"* (thanks a lot, pronounced MOO-chahs GRAH-see-ahs).

The blond lady rested her arm on Mama's shoulders and guided her toward the living room. "Now, come see what I found."

Carlos swung his leg onto the floor to make room for them on the couch, and Mrs. Peterson gave him something. *A book!* An adventure story about a boy in Hawaii. He couldn't help but smile at her. Tomorrow wouldn't be nearly as boring! He remembered to thank her before Mama could remind him.

Mrs. Peterson reached into her burgundy briefcase and pulled out a cardboard folder. It held several sheets of paper with columns of names on them, followed by rows of small

squares, also lined up in columns. "These are my Good
News Club attendance sheets from the past several years."
She held the top one for Mama (and Carlos) to see. "I have
various boxes after each child's name, and I make a check
in each one that applies to the child."

Mama looked confused and Carlos realized she didn't
understand much of what Mrs. Peterson said. He called for
Anna. She was better at interpreting than he was.

Anna walked into the living room after giving their
visitor a soft-spoken greeting (her eyes were red and puffy).
Mrs. Peterson explained the attendance sheets again,
waiting patiently while Anna changed her words to Spanish
for Mama.

"Do you see this column, labeled with a cross? That
means that if a child has a check in this box, he or she has
prayed to become a Christian. And I wouldn't check the
column unless I had talked with the child and felt assured
that he or she understood what being a Christian really
meant. Unless I knew that he or she *wanted* to be one."

She thumbed through the paper stack until she found a
sheet near the bottom that she pulled out and placed across
Mama's lap. She cleared her throat, and Carlos was amazed

to see tears in her eyes. "Take a look at the column after Luis' name...."

"Luis!" cried out Carlos in surprise.

Mrs. Peterson turned to him. "You don't remember that Luis was a member of my Good News Club, do you? When he was about your age. But you were only five years old, so you probably didn't understand—"

She was cut off by a gasp from Mama, who had clapped her hand over her mouth. Her shoulders began to shake. Mrs. Peterson wrapped her arms around her and Mama poured out muffled sobs. But they sounded different from the ones Carlos had heard escape her so often these past days. There was relief in them. And she kept murmuring, in Spanish, "Thank You, Lord Jesus! Thank You! I'll see my Luis again! I'll see him again!"

He reached for the attendance sheet. Mrs. Peterson guided Mama to the stuffed chair so Anna could sit beside Carlos. Then she handed them the list and the boy and girl bent over it together. The paper had turned creamy yellow and its corners were frayed. But there was his name, written in blue ink. Luis Hernandez. And there was the box, in the cross column. It had a check in it.

Anna gave a cry of joy. Carlos could only stare numbly. *He's all right. My brother was a Christian. He's in Heaven now.*

The boy felt relief, but not happiness. He was too ashamed for that. His own bitter words came back to him. *I don't believe in God anymore. He didn't answer my prayers. For all I know, Luis is lost . . . .*

He suddenly realized Mrs. Peterson was studying his face. "I *blew* it!" he blurted out. "I got angry at God for letting Luis die!"

She smiled, wiped her tears and spent the next half-hour explaining that God still loved him. She helped him realize that though he pulled away from Jesus, the Lord never abandoned him. And as they prayed together, Carlos knew deep inside that she was right.

"We may never know the answer, here on earth," she explained, when Carlos asked her why Luis had to die. "It breaks God's heart when people hurt each other—kill each other. It makes Him angry. He *will* see to it that Luis' killer is punished; if not here on earth, then someday when He judges the whole world."

"I can't wait to see that!" exulted Carlos, picturing the Blade who shot his brother cowering before Jesus as He condemned him forever.

"Oh, but Jesus loves the young man who shot Luis," Mrs. Peterson reminded him. "Just as much as He loves you. And His greatest desire is for him to become a Christian *before* that day of judgment, so he won't be punished forever. That's what I'm going to pray for."

Mama seemed to have a little of her old energy back. She beckoned Mrs. Peterson to the table for a cup of coffee and some churros. Carlos had been snacking all afternoon (out of boredom) and wasn't hungry. High-pitched whines trickled in through the back door—Peppy, begging for companionship. He excused himself, hopped on his crutches and went outside to visit him.

The boy sat on the back steps and Peppy wriggled close. The dog lolled his tongue sideways out of his mouth in a smile of pleasure as his young master scratched his chest. And he sat patiently still and pawed Carlos' leg while the boy rested his head against his furry side and cried and cried.

14

Mashell ran in spite of blinding tears. So what if she tripped over something? She *deserved* pain. Carlos' angry words only made her more determined to warn Ricardo and the other young men in the posse. She raced toward their most likely meeting place: the park.

And there was no sign of them. She asked the moms and grandmas if they'd seen the teens. One of them said yes. "They looked mad enough to bite your head off," one of them said. "So I left well enough *alone*. I don't be needin' to get some *gang* sore at me."

"They ain't a *gang*. Anyway, did you see where they went?" Mashell asked her anxiously.

The woman shrugged. No one else could tell her as much. She stalked out of the park and steeled herself to walk-jog to the nearest posse member's house. If only she could remember where it was.

"Fern Street," she muttered to herself. "It was close to school." She was already out of breath. The thought of walking all that way made her feel achy all over. And what if no one was home?

Just move it! she ordered herself. If she kept going, somewhere, somehow, she'd run into Ricardo and his posse. It wasn't like they'd moved to Alaska. She broke into a trot.

The girl was nearing Fern Street when she spotted something in an alley a block away. Something brown. A car? And why was its front-end shape so familiar? Sort of curved around the headlights and low to the ground? It was a *Camaro! The* Camaro.

So she wasn't the only one searching for the posse! She stopped with a gasp and dived behind a scraggly evergreen bush, hoping the Blades hadn't seen her. Maybe she was too far away from them . . . .

Her heart rose to her throat as she heard car doors opening. The girl peeked through the branches and wanted to scream at what she saw: three red-jacketed teens, striding toward her! One—who seemed to be this little group's leader—was the Blade who had chased her and Anna through Frederick Douglass Junior High!

No question that they knew who she was and that they were out to get her. And no question about what she should do. She lunged from her hiding place like a rabbit chased by wolves and raced in the opposite direction, all her soreness forgotten as she pushed herself to her top speed.

"What's your *hurry,* Mashell?" shouted the leader. "We just wanna talk to you! Shoot the breeze, you know?"

What else you gonna shoot? she thought. She glanced over her shoulder. They were running too. She had a good head start, but they were nearly-grown men. *Lord, H-E-E-E-E-L-P!*

Panic made it hard for her to breathe. All she could do was hurtle along, taking in gasps of air that sounded like sobs—because they were. Mashell rounded the corner and nearly slammed into a light pole. A chubby woman wearing a bright-orange jumper was standing near a backyard shed, staring at the skinny girl tearing past her house. *"Lady!"* Mashell screeched in passing. "Call the *police!"*

The woman cupped a hand over her ear. *"Slow down,* child!" she bellowed. "What did you say?"

There was no time to explain. Two of the Blades had just come around the corner. Mashell could only scream and run even harder.

Where could she go? How could she escape? A tornado seemed to be whirling around her, howling in her ears, scrambling her thoughts. She could almost feel the Blades tackling her. Knocking her legs out from under her. Dragging her away. Or maybe she'd feel a bullet hit her back.

She had to go where lots of people were! The Blades wouldn't dare beat up a girl in public, would they? She turned another corner and had a jouncing, pounding impression of quiet houses with small, cluttered yards as she raced toward the street in the distance—Century Boulevard, with its rushing traffic and busy stores and restaurants. If she reached it, she'd be safe!

She wished she could pull the street toward her. Or that she could turn herself into a zooming rocket. How much longer could she run all-out? Her lungs felt like someone had lit a fire in them. Her heart seemed to be thumping through her whole body.

Mashell glanced behind her. They were much closer. They'd catch her before she reached Century. And where was the third teen? Her question was answered in the next second. The brown Camaro surged around the last corner and sped toward her.

"*N-o-o-o!*" she whimpered. The car was cutting her off. It would be past her in a moment. Then the driver would jump out and grab her.

She couldn't turn back, or she'd run into the arms of the other two. So she shot to the left, hoping and praying she wouldn't wind up trapped in someone's yard.

The nearest one was surrounded by a waist-high wooden fence that she half-leaped, half-rolled over. *Somebody be here! Somebody help me!*

But no one was home. She sailed past the house and was scrambling over the back fence when the Blades reached the front one. She looked back to see the leader hook his belt. He was jerked backward and up, then he fell sideways and his partner tripped over him. They wound up in a heap.

She didn't wait around to hear them swear. A gravel-lined alley ran alongside the yard. The girl tore down it, faster than ever. One more glance behind. They were up and running again, but they were far behind now.

Mashell wanted to shriek in triumph, except she had no extra breath to do it. She was beating them! She was outrunning them! She'd reach Century Boulevard yet! The same elation she'd felt when she clocked the best time for the seventh-graders' fifty-yard dash burst through her and made her feel like she could fly.

Until the third teen hurtled himself over somebody else's fence and planted himself in her path with his arms and legs spread-eagled. She shot left again, toward an asphalt driveway that led to a three-story, white brick apartment building. Maybe she could cut through its parking lot to reach Century Boulevard!

Mashell flew past its parked cars, then its Dumpsters, then—what was *this?* A door was opening! Without a moment's thought, she headed toward it and shoved past a surprised, silver-haired man wearing a white undershirt and jeans, who grunted some words at her that she was too frenzied to hear. She pushed the door shut, tested its handle—y*es!* It was *locked!*—then skidded on slippery tile along a dim hallway lined with doors. Century Boulevard was right through that door at the other end! She could see the street through its window!

And then the Blade leader slammed his face to the glass.
She shrieked and stopped. The other two homeboys were
beating on the back door's window, bellowing at the
befuddled man, who scuttled to one of the hallway doors,
fumbled with his keys, and disappeared in his apartment.

What could she *do?* The street door was obviously
locked; the leader was thumping it and rattling its handle.
A stairway angled down to it. She raced toward it, praying
he wouldn't get the door open as she sailed past it.

Mashell leaped up the steps two at a time, past the
second floor and the third, to a doorway marked "Roof. No
pets allowed." She shoved it open and burst out into
waning sunshine and traffic noise and birds singing.

The roof was a jigsaw puzzle of large concrete tiles with
black tar between them. Lawn chairs with their paint
peeling, revealing gray wood underneath, were scattered
about, along with some empty jars and soda pop bottles and
squashed cans. She quickly dropped behind the three-foot
wall that rimmed the roof. No *way* did she want to be seen
from the ground!

But there was nowhere to *hide,* here. She couldn't go
back inside, because the Blades would break in sooner or

later. She couldn't climb down, because they'd spot her,
even if she didn't break her neck falling. She crawled to the
nearest chair and dragged it to the door as quietly as she
could. She'd seen a TV show where the heroine kept her
attacker out by angling a chair on its back legs and jamming
its back under a doorknob.

It worked. She tried opening the door, but the chair legs
scraped and stuck on the tiles, and the door froze as though
it was pressed against a wall. The girl felt her spirits rise
until she heard the three Blades arguing down below.
"She's on the roof, man! I know she is!"

"Let's smash a window and get in there!"

"They're all covered with bars!"

"Let's climb, then! Up the drain pipe in back! It'll be
dark soon and nobody will see us."

The teen was right. Night was on its way. And she was
sitting here with her back against a white-painted brick wall,
completely trapped!

15

The back door opened and Carlos looked up to see Mrs. Peterson walking through it. She sat beside him on the steps and rested one arm across his shoulders (and stroked Peppy's ears with the other one). "You'll go on missing Luis for a long time," she murmured.

He stared at his lap. "How long?"

"All your life, probably. The ache in your heart is at its worst right now. As months go by, you'll feel it less until your days are normal again. But you'll never stop getting stung by twinges of grief. Something will remind you of him, like his birthday, or his favorite song. Or you'll hear somebody laugh like him. And all you can do is let the wave of hurt wash over you, then keep going with your life." She gave his back a pat. "And don't *ever* feel embarrassed about crying."

Had she heard him through an open window? He
decided to change the subject, to one he knew she'd latch on
to. "I'm glad I'm not angry at God no more."

She beamed. "I'm glad too! I'm glad you finally
realize that He'll *always* forgive you. And that He'll never
let you get away from Him."

Something was still bothering him. "I—gotta ask Jesus
to forgive me for what I said—to Mashell today. Some really
ugly things. Like, I blamed her for Luis getting killed. And
when she said she was sorry, I didn't forgive her."

The lady gave him a shocked frown. "How could *she*
have had anything to do with Luis' death?"

Carlos told her about Mashell's lie and Luis bursting in
on the girls and finding out the name of the wannabe Blade
who shot Rudy and the homeboy who shot *him.* Mrs.
Peterson, obviously upset, spluttered, "But as angry as Luis
was, don't you think he would have gone out gunning for a
Blade whether he knew who shot you or not?"

Her cheeks were getting red, and she spoke faster and
faster. "And maybe the Blades were out to get him *first.*"

Her words brought a horrible thought to his mind.
Something Mashell had said that didn't sink in. Until now.
He struggled to his feet. *"Hold on!* She tried to warn me

that the Blades *were* out to get the posse! And I was so
mad, I didn't *listen* to her, you know?" His voice went soft.
"I bet they were out to get Luis too!"

He felt relieved and he wasn't sure why. Maybe
because he'd been blaming himself for his brother's death,
as well. But heavy fear quickly smothered his peace. "Mrs.
Peterson, Mashell came to my house to warn Ricardo that
the Blades were out to get *him! All* the guys in the posse!"

His first impulse was to start running toward the park,
the posse's most likely meeting place. He forgot about his
broken leg for a split-second—long enough to nearly topple
off the steps. Mrs. Peterson clutched his shoulders and
steadied him.

"Calm down!" she ordered him.

"I've got to find Ricardo or he'll die too!"

"You don't have to do anything but stay home and pray.
Your job is to keep *safe."*

"But what about Mashell? I gotta find her! I gotta tell
her it wasn't her fault. She ran away crying, you know?
She asked me to forgive her and I didn't do it!"

Mrs. Peterson took a deep breath. "And if I know that
girl, she's tearing around Watts trying to make everything

right." Anxiety showed in her eyes, in spite of her efforts to act calm.

There was only one way to find out what she'd really done. "Can I ride with you to Mashell's house?"

The silvery-blond lady was unwilling, at first. But Carlos used every ploy he knew to change her mind—and Mama's too. He begged and used logic and gave promises until both women reluctantly gave in. Anna was busy setting the table for supper. She caught his eye and he saw worry mixed with yearning for him to succeed. Did she know what he had in mind? That he planned to coax Mrs. Peterson into searching for Ricardo and his friends?

Yeah. She knew.

He sat sideways with his leg stretched across the minivan's middle seat (which meant the seat belt dug into his hip). Mrs. Peterson stopped in front of Mashell's living unit at Gordon Brown. The girl wasn't home. Not that he expected her to be there.

Mashell's mom, Carolyn Robertson, nearly blasted his ears off when she learned her daughter was running around Watts trying to stop teenage boys from fighting each other. "That girl! I *swear* she gonna be the death of me!" She started to mock her daughter's voice. " 'I gotta comfort Anna! I'll come straight home, Mom!' Yeah, *right!* All I can say is, she in *big* trouble now!"

What she'd just said registered on her face. "I gotta find my baby before she gets herself *killed!*"

Carlos could hardly look the woman in the face as he told her it was his anger that drove Mashell to this desperate search. "When I find her, I'm gonna ask her to forgive *me.*"

Mrs. Peterson volunteered to drive Carolyn around Watts until they found her daughter. She accepted her offer. Carlos wriggled onto the van seat and buckled in as quietly as he could. The two ladies weren't taking much notice of him, which was exactly what he wanted.

"How about the park, first?" suggested Mrs. Peterson.

Yeah! The park! thought Carlos eagerly.

Both women questioned people as Carlos sat in the minivan and scanned every tree and teeter-totter for a sign of Mashell or Ricardo or the posse or even the Blades. Nothing.

Mrs. Peterson hopped back into her driver's seat and informed them she'd met a woman who thought she'd spoken to Mashell. But who had no idea where the girl had gone.

"If she's looking for Ricardo, she'll go to his friends' houses," said Carlos. "Like, the closest guy lives near my school on Fern Street."

Mrs. Peterson gave him an irate glance over her shoulder. "I shouldn't let you come along. But I don't know how else we'll find our way around. You know Ricardo and his buddies, and I don't."

Carlos kept himself from grinning into the rearview mirror. No sense pushing his luck. He was being allowed on the search, which was everything he hoped for. Other than finding Mashell and Ricardo and seeing them both at home, safe.

They heard exciting (and scary) news at the first posse member's house. The teenager's mother hadn't seen Mashell, but she told them her son had just left with three of his friends in an old Ford pickup truck.

Carlos rolled down the minivan's window to listen. "A *green* truck?" he yelled. "With rust and dents all over it?"

"*Si*," answered the lady.

"Was my brother, Ricardo Hernandez, with them?"

She thought so. She had no idea where they were going.

Mrs. Peterson looked into the mirror as she started the

minivan. "Now hold on, Carlos. We're not searching for your brother right now. We're searching for *Mashell.*"

"But he might get *killed!*"

"We're not driving into the middle of a street battle!"

She glanced again. It must have been the terror and pleading on his face that removed her hand from the ignition key. "I'll have that boy's mother call the police," she said softly as she pushed her door open.

They were on their way again in a few minutes. Carlos could hardly sit still and steadily tapped the seat back with his fingertips until Mashell's mom asked him not-so-politely to stop. They reached Century Boulevard. "Turn right," said Carlos. "Another one of the guys lives along here." He added hastily, "And Mashell probably knows that."

Mrs. Peterson made the turn, and Carlos frantically scanned the apartment buildings and restaurants and stores along the street, hoping he'd spot Mashell or a green pickup full of teenagers.

The sun was close to setting, which made fences and buildings and even crumpled cans and paper wads glow orange on the sides facing the rays. The shadows were long and black and stark. He prayed they'd find Mashell and his brother before night fell. And before something terrible happened.

* * * * * * * *

Mashell kept imagining she heard a Blade scrabbling up the back drain pipe. But not yet, she knew. Not until darkness covered them like a blanket from the devil.

She wished she knew what they wanted her for. Questioning? As a hostage? Or just to make an example of her to the posse? She couldn't help but cry, out of fear and dread.

The girl prayed feverishly, and thought and thought. Maybe she should scream at somebody passing by and ask them to call the police. But what would keep the Blades from climbing up that instant and dragging her away before the police could get there? Maybe she could throw jars at them and knock them out. But the thought made her feel sick. And what if she missed? Or only knocked *one* out? Then they'd *really* be angry with her.

At last she decided to sneak back inside the building and bang on doors until somebody let her in. The thought of trusting a complete stranger terrified her, but *anything* was better than getting caught by the Blades! She scuttled to the stairway door on all fours like a crab.

But the door wouldn't budge! *No!* She'd jammed the chair against it too tightly! She kicked it, shoved it, jumped on it.... Nothing worked. She wound up wiping tears—of frustration this time.

She forced herself to peek over the roof wall. The girl had to look hard to see the three teens, with their red jackets and their slicked-back hair and their knife tattoos barely showing above their muscle shirts. But they were there, like wolves waiting for the moon to rise so they could start their nightly hunt.

Suddenly the leader jumped from his hiding place and pointed toward the street. He hissed something that drew the others out, too. What was he so excited about?

Mashell saw a green pickup going by, with two teenage boys in the cab and two more in back. *Wait!* Wasn't one of them....

Ricardo! She wanted to scream his name, as if he'd hear her. She watched in horror as the leader pulled a fierce-looking black handgun from a holster under his jacket and took aim at the truck.

"NO!" she screamed. Mashell lunged for the nearest jar (it was covered with a greasy, beige smog-film) and threw it at him. It smashed near his feet and he flinched and swore.

She'd kept him from shooting for a few seconds, anyway. But this was no time to exult. The teen, full of rage, had turned to face her. He brought the gun up and aimed it at her head! She ducked behind the wall with a gasp of fright as the blast *cracked* and echoed off the buildings around her.

The other Blades called him foul names and demanded to know what he'd done *that* for. "Stupid waste!" they yelled, among other things. But now she heard a screech of brakes and truck doors slamming. More shots burst from the three guns below her. And answering fire carried from across the street. It all happened so fast. Faster than she could blink.

She could easily guess what was happening. The posse, including Ricardo, had stopped the truck. The battle had begun. She covered her face. What if Ricardo died? Why didn't he—why didn't all of them—just give it *up?*

It took all her courage to peek over the wall again (in a completely different place than the section that had a fresh gouge from a bullet on its curved top.) She saw the leader and dropped down again in a hurry. But he and his friends were too busy to shoot her, at the moment. The girl looked again. They were spread out below her, two of them kneeling behind a bus bench and one leaning against a concrete column, guns ready, tense, alert.

She could see Ricardo and his friends squatting behind the pickup. Both sides of the war had already stymied each other. For a few minutes, anyway. She wondered how long it would be before someone jumped from his hiding place to become a target.

Traffic kept roaring by, but pedestrians stopped with fright on their faces and ducked into buildings or hurried in the direction they'd come. *Where were the police?*

"Hernandez!" shouted the leader. "Quick! Look at the roof! You see the top of a little head peeking over the wall?"

Mashell clapped her hand over her mouth and hunkered down. *Girl, are you stupid! Why you have to be so curious?*

"It's Mashell Robertson. You know her? One of your little brother's friends? We chased her, but she's a pretty fast runner. She got herself onto the roof of that building, but now she's trapped. We plan to make her an honorary

Blade before we kill her. Pretty good plan, huh?"

Ricardo raised a shout, in a voice tight with worry. "Are you really up there, Mashell?"

What should she *do?* Keep quiet? The Blades were only trying to lure Ricardo out into the open so they could shoot him. But what if the posse went away and she really *did* fall into the Blades' hands?

"Yeah!" she yelled, and was sure she heard a groan from across the street. She wanted to punch herself in the ribs for getting herself into this situation. If Ricardo or anybody else died, it would be her fault *again.*

"You better come out and fight us if you want to get her back," said the leader. "Show us your face, Hernandez. Come on, man! Or are you too scared?"

Mashell stared wildly around the roof. She had to *do* something before the battle erupted again. Maybe she could drive the Blades from *their* shelters! Make *them* go out into the open! She grabbed bottles and flung them over the wall, taking care never to let her head rise above it.

They clinked and shattered. But no new shots rang out. "You're missing us by a mile," the leader informed her.

She gritted her teeth in frustration. Wasn't she throwing the bottles in the direction of their voices? If only she dared peer over the side, so she could aim!

"More to your right, Mashell!" bellowed Ricardo. "And throw harder!"

She actually grinned as she followed his instructions. But the leader's next words filled her with fear. "Go get her."

The girl heard rapid footsteps. Several guns went off at once. The runner paused, probably at the next thing to duck behind. Then those awful steps began again. She heard wild shouts. More pistol blasts. More running.

The water pipe began to quiver. The Blade was climbing.

Carlos caught sight of the green pickup and let out a
yell. Mrs. Peterson swung the minivan to the curb and
stopped with a squeal of brakes. But she refused to let him
out. "They *shootin'* each other!" shouted Carolyn
Robertson. "Get us *away* from here!"

Mrs. Peterson wrenched the steering wheel. She was
going to pull a U-turn. But she had to wait for a space in
the traffic first. Carlos saw his chance.

He unbuckled himself, grabbed his crutches, squirmed
to the door and punched it open.

He leaped to the sidewalk on his good leg, ignoring Mrs.
Peterson's shouts. *Nothing* was going to keep him from
saving his brother!

"Ricardo!"

He shoved himself forward on his crutches with all the strength in his arms. Suddenly a large somebody lunged at him from beside a car. Strong arms wrapped around his waist and tackled him to the ground, but gently, breaking his fall. At the same instant, he heard a gun go off, and a bullet *pinged* off something metal.

"Carlos, you little *fool!*" babbled Ricardo. "You wanna get shot in the *head* this time?"

They sat up together and the boy wrapped his arms tight around his brother's neck. "I don't want you to die! I don't want you to die! You gotta stop fighting! You gotta forgive those guys! *Please!* If you die, it won't bring Luis back! And maybe one of those Blades has a little brother too! I don't want you to kill anybody! I don't want you to—*die!*"

He rested his head on Ricardo's shoulders and broke down into too hard a cry to get any more words out. His brother wrapped his arms around him and held him close, pulling one arm away only long enough to wipe his own tears. His three friends had taken shelter behind the same car. "You heard him guys," Ricardo finally managed to say to them in a half-whisper. "Let's stop fighting."

"But those *asesinos* are still out to get us!" protested one of them.

As if in answer, they heard the wavering wail of sirens, far away but rapidly getting closer. Carlos looked up in time to see three red-jacketed teens across the street, running away as fast as they could. One of them limped and held his head.

"Why didn't you get her? She could have been our *hostage!*" he heard one of them shout.

He barely made out the injured one's answer as the three of them rounded the corner at the end of the block. *"Because, man!* Every time I started climbing, she dropped a chair on me!"

Ricardo and his friends suddenly burst into loud laughter. Carlos had no idea what was so funny, but he found himself giggling too. Ricardo's laugh had always been contagious.

* * * * * * * *

Carlos hooked the chain leash onto Peppy's leather collar. The dog was so eager to run, he hop-squirmed in a circle until the chain wrapped around his young master's legs. "Hold *still!*" he ordered him with a grunt of disgust.

He stared at his right leg as he untwisted himself from the leash. It looked *funny.* Pale, hairy, skinny. When the doctor had taken the cast off yesterday, it felt as though his leg floated to the ceiling, now that all that weight was gone. "It's looking *good!*" the doctor bragged as he stared at the surgery scar. "You've healed very well."

He wished his heart healed as fast. He still could hardly think of Luis without choking up. And he thought about him all the time. He was *deeply* glad about one thing: the Blade that had shot Luis—Mashell kept calling him "the leader"—was in jail now, awaiting his trial for murder. Carlos forced himself to pray for him—that he'd learn about Jesus' love. But it wasn't easy. *Lord, I forgive him,* the boy kept telling God. *Will my anger go away with time, just like my sadness?*

He decided all he could do was wait and see. The police not only caught the three Blades who tried to kidnap Mashell and wipe out Ricardo's posse, but they blitz-raided the houses of other homeboys. All in one night they arrested dozens of Blades, Knights and other gang members. They found handguns and rifles and knives and illegal drugs. And got them and their users off the streets for awhile.

The teens in the posse threw away their weapons. Ricardo, to honor his brother, went to the alley where he'd been killed and painted roses on the concrete, surrounding these words scrawled in white spray paint: "Luis Hernandez. DOA." Which stood for "dead on arrival."

Papa planted a rose bush on his grave, and Carlos put silk blossoms on it to keep the site blooming until the real flowers opened. The boy took the soccer ball Luis and Ricardo had given him and placed it on top of his dresser. He'd never play with it. He'd keep it as reminder of his brother.

All Carlos had to do now was wait for life to return to "normal." Except that Mama and Anna still cried out loud a lot. Papa had a sorrow in his eyes that never went away. Ricardo didn't say much these days, either. He and Luis had been as close as best friends. Even the little girls played more quietly, and not as much. The only cheerful members of the Hernandez family were Rosa and Peppy.

Who was dragging his young master toward the front sidewalk, snorting with excitement and gagging as he strained against the backward pull of his collar. Carlos broke into a run, just to keep the dog from choking himself.

His leg felt pretty good—a little sore, maybe. He guided Peppy to the park and was surprised to see a group of kids gathered at the playing field. The moms around here must have finally let them back in the park. Of course, it was a safer place now. Carlos heard a familiar voice shouting at him.

"Hola, man! You got your cast off! *When?"*

Felipe ran toward him, patted Peppy's head and gave his friend a huge grin. Carlos didn't feel like smiling back. "Yesterday."

"Why didn't you *tell* me? I woulda got you out here to play. We *need* you, man!"

Because I don't want to! thought Carlos. *I don't ever wanna play again!*

"Why can't he join in now?" piped up Mashell. (Most of the Good News Club had gathered around. She was smiling too. He'd asked her to forgive him over a month ago, and she'd willingly done it.)

Jose, the other team's captain, had been listening in. "You can't add a new player when the game's almost half over!"

Felipe glowered at him. "Who *says?*"

"Give 'im a *break!* He just got his cast off!" said Mashell hotly.

Jose folded his arms. "He says he doesn't wanna play with *foul-mouthed cheaters,* anyway."

Comments like "Oh, come *on!*" and "Don't be such a *baby!*" burst out of the Good News Club. Jose scowled at them and stuck his chest out. Carlos saw a fight coming. And he knew how to stop it—with something he'd planned to say, anyway. He would have liked privacy . . . .

"Jose, I'm sorry I insulted you. I shouldn't have said what I said."

Jose's eyes opened wide in surprise. His tight muscles relaxed and his chest sank as though it was a balloon that someone popped. "I—uh—you . . . ." His voice trailed away and he stared at the ground. The other kids stood silent.

"Will you forgive me?" Carlos continued.

Jose looked up with a flushed face. "Yeah . . . sure, man."

"But what if he really *was* cheating?" put in Felipe.

Jose winced. "I—if I did trip you that time we were playing wallball, I didn't really—I mean, I didn't *really* wanna trip you. I—didn't think. I—I really hate to *lose,* you know? I'm—sorry."

"I forgive you."

Carlos almost laughed at the relief all over Jose's face and body—like invisible chains twisted around him had suddenly fallen off. The boy gave him a wide grin. "Let's play some *ball,* man!"

Before he could say no, Carlos found himself placed fourth in the hitting order. His teammates slapped his shoulders and hoped out loud that the three players ahead of him would get on base. "Then you'll hit a grand slam home run!" exulted Felipe.

Carlos wasn't so sure. He hadn't played for over two months! Could he still hit the ball as hard as they expected him to?

He'd have to wait to find out. The first hitter made a double out (they had one out already), and the Good News Club had to take the field. Carlos tied Peppy's leash to a bench leg, then trudged to second base, wondering if his out-of-practice hands would let him catch balls and tag

runners. The first one up for the other team was a seven-
year-old girl (Jose's younger sister), who made such a tiny
hit that she reached first just because Mashell, playing
shortstop, couldn't scramble forward fast enough. (They
didn't have catchers. The first-base player usually ran in to
cover if someone was tearing toward home.)

Carlos found himself shouting orders to the other
players. And cheering when Felipe caught the next hitter's
ball in midair for the first out. Tamyra was up. She thunked
the ball hard, but Mashell backed up and fielded it on the
first bounce. Carlos didn't need to yell at her. He knew she
knew what to do. He planted his left foot on second base.
She flung the ball hard at his chest. He caught it, whirled
and threw the ball in a perfect straight line to Felipe,
covering first.

The seven-year-old girl was only halfway to second.
Tamyra hadn't reached first, either. *"Double play!"* he
bellowed. His team whooped and hollered. He joined them.
As they trotted off the field, Mashell raced over and slapped
hands with him. He was grinning as hard as she was.

The two hitters ahead of him made it safely to first and
second. (An outfielder dropped the ball, which definitely

helped.) "All right, man!" said Felipe in a low voice. "You can give us three more points here. Then we'll only be two behind. *Pound* it, you know?"

He knew. Carlos strolled to home plate, reveling in the thumping heart and wild excitement he'd felt so often before. Everybody on the other team backed up. As if it would do them any good.

Control, he reminded himself. *Don't get so excited you lose control.*

He sized up the outfield and decided to aim toward the right. He held the ball on his outstretched hand, took a deep breath, bored his eyes into it, and—

"Hrrnngg!" Hit it as hard as he ever had in his life. He couldn't help but yell with joy as he tore around the bases. He'd reached home before the other team could even get the ball into the infield. The Good News Club squealed and cheered and slapped him on the back.

And then, to his surprise, he heard another voice cheering. A deep voice. Certainly not a kid's. He looked in the voice's direction.

"Hey, Ricardo!" he answered, giving his brother a wave. Ricardo whispered something to his friends (five members of the *former* posse). The six teens formed a line and bellowed, all at the same time, "The fistball star is *back!*"

They turned it into a rhythmic chant that they walk-danced and clapped to. The Good News Club picked up on it and soon they had a sort of rap parade going around the park. Carlos sat on the bench and chuckled and scratched Peppy's back and wondered when his red-hot face would cool off.

And suddenly he realized he was feeling happy.

The teens went somewhere else, and Jose got the game started again. Carlos was glad everyone's attention was off him because he had a few loose tears to blink away. The sight of Ricardo laughing with his friends only made him miss Luis even more. But he was also as glad as *anything* that Ricardo was still alive. How much worse would it hurt to have no brothers left at all?

He realized how much he loved Ricardo and his family and even his friends. (His face was getting warm again.) And Peppy, who was lying on his feet so that his toes were going numb.

He focused back onto the game and prayed that his friends in the Good News Club—*all* the kids playing fistball, on both teams—would stay out of the gangs. If they did that—if they chose to be friends instead of enemies—then their part of the street wars would end. Maybe friendship would spread all over Los Angeles.

Then he could look forward to more adventures without being scared to go on the streets. No other girls would get chased by homeboys like Mashell had been. No other boys would lose their older brothers.

Please God! Let it be!

Get a Life!

This life is short, you know—and full of trouble. That's because *we all* have a problem called sin. We do bad things that break God's laws, like lying, cheating and having mean thoughts. And because God is holy—He never does wrong—sin keeps us away from Him. That's a bad situation because the punishment for sin is to be away from God *forever*.

But there's a good side. The Bible says, "God so loved the world that he gave his one and only Son, that whoever believes in him shall not perish but have eternal life" (John 3:16). God loves *you*. That's why Jesus Christ, God's Son, died on the cross to pay for *your* sins. Three days after they buried Him, He came back to life and today He's in Heaven. That's where He wants *you* to be someday. When you trust Him to save you from your sins, He does it. Would you like Jesus to forgive you right now? Go ahead and talk to Him. You can pray something like this:

Dear God, I believe You sent Jesus to die for me. I'm sorry for the wrong things I've done. Please take away my sin and help me live a new life. Thank You for being my absolutely best, Forever Friend. Amen.

If you just trusted Jesus to save you, you have a new life inside you. This would be a great time to join a Good News Club to learn more about your new life. Call 1-800-300-4033 to find out more.

174